GW00372040

PRAISE FOR *CULTURE SHIFT*

'The mix of personal experience and straight-talking advice creates a vital handbook for anyone taking on the task of managing culture.'

SUNNY VARKEY, *Founder of GEMS Education and Varkey Foundation*

'I taught culture at a business school for years, and always felt that I was about to get found out, because all the models I came across sounded plausible but simply didn't work. I wish I'd had this book, and I wish I'd written it. Bravo – it should be issued to all new leaders along with their security pass on day one.'

EVE POOLE, *author of* Leadersmithing

'Culture is so fundamental to peformance, and yet working to improve it often attracts myth, mystery and scepticism. Seen on the one hand as the intangible soft stuff, or on the other as something simplistically to be fixed, neither approach will be successful. This books finds a way through the middle, based on real experience and outcomes. It's straight talking, realistic and refreshingly honest. And it's proven. I know – I worked closely with the author in some of the case studies referenced. If you are approaching the topic of driving change through culture, start here with this book. It will help you make sense of a topic so often avoided, yet so essential to grasp.'

IAIN CONN, *CEO Centrica Plc*

'One person's logic is not another's – a key premise of this accessible book that unpicks why you can't simply announce the culture you want, and expect to create it. It takes time, effort, balance and a healthy dose of pig-headedness. Wonderful, original stuff.'

CHARLIE HODGSON, *Team and Leadership Coach*

CULTURE SHIFT

CULTURE SHIFT

A Practical Guide to Managing Organizational Culture

KIRSTY BASHFORTH

BLOOMSBURY BUSINESS

LONDON · NEW YORK · OXFORD · NEW DELHI · SYDNEY

BLOOMSBURY BUSINESS
Bloomsbury Publishing Plc
50 Bedford Square, London, WC1B 3DP, UK
1385 Broadway, New York, NY 10018, USA

BLOOMSBURY, BLOOMSBURY BUSINESS and the Diana logo are trademarks of
Bloomsbury Publishing Plc

First published in Great Britain 2019

Copyright © Kirsty Bashforth, 2019

Cover design by Jason Anscomb/Rawshock Designs

Kirsty Bashforth has asserted her right under the Copyright, Designs and Patents Act,
1988, to be identified as Author of this work.

All rights reserved. No part of this publication may be reproduced or transmitted
in any form or by any means, electronic or mechanical, including photocopying,
recording, or any information storage or retrieval system, without prior permission
in writing from the publishers.

Bloomsbury Publishing Plc does not have any control over, or responsibility for, any
third-party websites referred to or in this book. All internet addresses given in this
book were correct at the time of going to press. The author and publisher regret
any inconvenience caused if addresses have changed or sites have ceased to
exist, but can accept no responsibility for any such changes.

A catalogue record for this book is available from the British Library.

A catalog record for this book is available from the Library of Congress.

ISBN: HB: 978-1-4729-6620-9
       ePDF: 978-1-4729-6622-3
       eBook: 978-1-4729-6621-6

Typeset by RefineCatch Limited, Bungay, Suffolk
Printed and bound in Great Britain

To find out more about our authors and books visit www.bloomsbury.com
and sign up for our newsletters.

SURREY LIBRARIES	
Askews & Holts	26-Jul-2019
658.406 ECO	£20.00

For

David, George & Freddie

CONTENTS

PREFACE

Why this book is needed

'Culture eats strategy for breakfast' – that over-used nugget of wisdom, never more fashionable in the business world than in the aftermath of the global financial crisis. But do people really understand what that means, and more importantly, how to make it happen?

A common practice in too many businesses (especially large, established ones) is to see culture change as a project, with a start and an end; to hand it to someone in HR, to bring in a team of consultants who will use data analytics and textbook models to define today's culture and outline tomorrow's required state, and then create and track a perfect plan of activity to drive towards that end state. After 6–12 months, they will have delivered their brief, and while there will be an observable shift in behaviour in the organization – for the duration that the focus remains overt – many will continue the way they have always worked. Either way, once the project is considered 'done', the dominant culture re-emerges and things go back to how they were.

This book is about how to do things differently, so that the culture really does shift. It's about the very top leadership owning their work and using their own talent from the line to lead it. No external consultants, minimal budget (if any), setting goals not plans, direction not precision, and putting the culture work at the core of running the business, on an ongoing basis; not just as a one-off 'fix'.

Managing culture in an organization is neither as creative and unbounded as an art, nor is it as precise and as empirically evidenced as a science.

It is a craft: a blend of the two. And it's challenging and rewarding work.

I want to encourage you to turn traditional thinking on its head – whichever way you would normally approach this, we're going to learn how to do the opposite.

Who's the audience?

This book is for anyone who has the responsibility to shift the culture of an organization:

- From CEOs to employees: individuals who have been handed the task by someone more senior.

- For sceptics: I will explain how culture makes a difference, how change can be made, and how it's more than 'just HR professionals hugging trees'. Culture is the core of business and this book will show you why, and how to make sense of it, manage it and shift it.

- For aspiring leaders: to those who think they have been given an impossible task, I will explain how establishing a culture is actually the greatest opportunity available. The ability to see the whole company, to influence its future, and to work closely with the top team – as well as across the organization – sets you up for the future and ensures you have a legacy. It's challenging, insightful and hugely rewarding.

- For the human resources manager: I will show you how to fight HR-sceptics and stop pushing water uphill, by ensuring your colleagues are leading the push from the frontline.

- And for the change agent: the individual who's tried everything and is out of ideas, but willing to give it one more shot. This book is full of ideas to help you think differently, break eggs, stop following plans, and go for it. It won't be easy (you're used to that), but you will be able to make a difference and you will be valued.

This book will show you how the person overseeing this work should be the air-traffic controller, not the pilot of the plane. This analogy is fundamental to managing and shifting a culture sustainably.

Anyone who has ever tried to lead a shift in behaviour will know that telling a person how to behave only causes them to react against you. Instead, your role is to be the architect of the environment, channelling the workforce into a certain way of behaving, and ensuring that the behaviour that is required becomes the norm. You are not telling the pilot how to fly the plane or flying it yourself, but are creating the clear environment in which they can fly and land safely, *without* crashing into others. It's fundamental that you become an expert at setting those parameters, scanning the environment for potential threats, misalignment and weak signals. Others have to trust you to accomplish this, and in return you have to trust them to do their job. Setting expectations together is vital here.

Within these pages I will explain how to hold the whole picture, the environment, and how to see dynamics play out from all the different angles and stakeholders. I will explain how to set the parameters in order for the shift to happen, and how to ensure individuals trust that you comprehend the bigger picture and have the skills and credibility to direct the process, without having to micromanage their jobs or priorities. I will give you the tools and knowledge, so you are equipped with the authority to ensure others operate within those parameters, while the boundary of your remit remains clear.

Why is it different and why now?

This is not a book full of academic models about organizational culture, but a practical guide about how to shift and manage one. It is based on 28 years' experience of corporate life, with five years of leading a shift in work culture in an organization of 80,000 people in 80 countries.

And now is the prime time for you to discover it.

Behavioural economics is finally, and rightly, emerging into the daylight of established practice, with the 2017 Nobel Prize for Economics going to Richard Thaler and his work on the topic.

As this guide is founded on behavioural economics, it recognises that people do not make 'average' assumptions and do not always (or often) follow what others may view as rational logic. Shifting and managing a culture is thus not about telling people what to do and expecting them to neatly fall in line, but about recognising where they really are and how they make decisions; all so that you can start to shift the environment, influencing them to make different decisions and form new habits.

Finally, I challenge in this book that culture does not, in fact, eat strategy for breakfast – rather, it is its equal and inextricably linked partner. One doesn't trump the other; they have to work in partnership, on an equal footing to enable the best performance to be delivered. A machine needs both the engine at peak tuning and the right fuel to operate it well. It's a symbiotic relationship, and it's the same with culture and strategy.

NOTE FROM THE AUTHOR

Please tell me it's not another business school model

This book is written from experience; it's not a theoretical exercise, and it's not from academic study (although my love of economics, what with my degree and emerging fascination with behavioural economics, have played an integral part).

This knowledge stems from what I've learnt throughout my career in a global, multinational business, in addition to running my own business and being on the boards of others.

It is the culmination of 28 years of commercial experience and recognising that a clear purpose and strong strategy are not sufficient. The way people work together, behave, make decisions, how they perceive and interpret what is right or wrong – the culture – makes or breaks business success, whether that is in the short term or the longer term.

Through trial and a notable amount of error, what you find within these pages is what I have personally discovered works when it comes to organizational culture. Not to say that I have totally cracked this obstacle, however I do recognise when I am onto something.

Too much value is wasted or worse, destroyed, when culture is not governed or managed as a business asset alongside others. In essence, this is a handbook for anyone wanting to do better in this area, but who may not know where to start.

Culture is my business and at QuayFive we equip Chairmen, Boards, CEOs, Executive Management Teams and Change leads to:

- effectively diagnose and reflect on current culture
- put organizational culture at the heart of business planning and management
- align organizational culture with strategy and purpose to drive sustained performance
- and be able to do it for themselves, without external help.

Handbook hashtags

As it has already been stated: this is not an academic book; it's a handbook.

What this means is that it is intended to be practical and useable in day to day work; something that can be picked up and turned to, if ever you encounter a roadblock or discover that something is simply not working.

I do not aim to lecture readers on the merits of one model over another. Each chapter is a step to both help you to deliver more, and to give you confidence that you are on the right track.

With this in mind, I have tried to headline the various sections with titles that act as a shorthand for the key point being made. In my corporate life, I have always tried to get inside employees' heads and work from that perspective – to imagine the information they might be receiving, and what they choose to do about it as a result, rather than prioritising my own perspective on what *I* think they should know.

This is reflected in the way I title emails, or structure presentations, and I have applied the same principle here. How do I sum up what's inside; how can I encourage people to read it; how do I make it clear, interesting, or at least something to catch the eye? And most importantly, how can I keep it concise?

So I have chosen to start each chapter, and each section, with a short title that sums up the core idea. Think of it as a handbook hashtag.

And at the end of each chapter you will also find the key points summed up in 'at a glance', acting as a simple reminder, a list or a trigger to what you need to remember when it's all boiled down.

Not timeless, but not a snapshot

Clearly my thinking and experience emanates from the era in which I have been leading such work, and it therefore has its own context that in 20 years may look a little retro. At the same time, I have found that common sense and an understanding of what makes people tick are two core foundations of what works in the world of organizational culture.

Which means much of this knowledge should endure.

I have tried to use examples to illustrate key points, but to also relate these scenarios with the reader's own experiences, rather than solely focusing on particular company headline events. Peppering the latter throughout the book was an enticing prospect to bring it to life, but would have left the handbook 'stuck in time' and soon out of touch.

Introduction

What is culture?

'Culture is what happens when the CEO isn't in the room'
JOHN COLLISON, CEO Stripe

Culture is the sum total of the way we think, interact and behave in an organization. It is the pervasive character of the business, through everyone's perceptions, language and actions. Its core should include a clear sense of purpose and shared values that guide decision-making across the company.

Source: Entrepreneur.com

'a blend of the values, beliefs, taboos, symbols, rituals and myths all companies develop over time'

In other words, company culture is the personality of an organization from the employee perspective, and includes the company's mission, expectations and work atmosphere. Whether it's written down, symbolized in the business logo, or simply an unspoken but understood definition, culture determines a company's environment

---

Culture is hard to pin down: when it runs smoothly, you know it; when it works against you, that becomes evident too. Nonetheless, it remains difficult to define. You can see culture in the moments when no one has to issue instructions, because people just know how to accomplish a goal, or when people make decisions under stress, or when customers and clients summarise their experience with a firm and its employees.

Culture is not simply the processes and policies in which we are required to operate, but the language people use, the networks, habits and norms they adopt to get work done, who they perceive is in charge, how decisions are made, the key influences on the psyche in the organization, and more. In culture, myths and fables are just as crucial as facts and figures.

It's also important to note that an effective culture shouldn't be confused with a 'nice' culture, a great brand or a team full of clones:

- An organization can be a lovely place to work, but underperforming and ineffective given what it's trying to achieve. Eventually it runs out of road.

- A brand can be hugely powerful but have a dysfunctional culture, unaligned with the vision: after a while this comes to the surface.

- Groupthink is a dangerous place to be, as it can lead to a lack of awareness of impending risks and opportunities, with challenge increasingly seen as a lack of cultural fit, or too disruptive.

An effective culture is one where your culture enables and reinforces your strategy delivery and your brand communication. Employees interact, behave and make decisions daily, within an overall guiding compass of ethos. Like the words through a stick of confectionery rock, the culture is the message every stakeholder experiences, inseparable from every bite. Culture is 'the way things really work around here'.

No two cultures are identical; you can't clone one, and you wouldn't want to. Because remember that culture consists of human behaviour. However, you can find defining characteristics that tend to place organizational cultures into different categories, examples including:

Examples of different categories of culture

Team-first

Engaged employees with the freedom to choose, space to operate and flexibility to prioritise, stay longer with the organization, deliver better customer experience and have higher productivity. That's the rationale. Hiring is based on cultural fit, and the wellbeing of the team is all. Employees are the focus and at the centre of the organization's policies.

⇨ *Southwest Airlines*

Elite

Changing the world, breaking new ground, disrupting the market, redefining what's possible – just pick one of these as the mission. Only the best employees are hired, with no compromise. These organizations are impatient and don't wait for anyone, least of all their employees, who they expect to be leading the charge. They are pre-disposed to risk-taking.

⇨ *Ryanair, Uber, Space-X*

Horizontal

Collaboration and cooperation are the foundation. They communicate across teams, openly and constantly. It's all about the sharing. This does not mean a lack of structure, but that titles are not as important. Instead, ideas come from everywhere and anywhere, with teams fluidly working together to tackle a problem.

⇨ *Google*

Conventional

Clearly defined hierarchies and roles, finding new forms of communication a challenge in this changing environment. CEO still takes lots of big decisions.

- *Outcome: all about the results. Performance management is the lifeblood, set around measurable objectives, key indicators and rewards tied back to these for each individual. If it's not measurable, it's not part of performance.*

  ⇨ *BP*

  ⇨ *Toyota in the 80s/90s*

Of course, every organization has a mix of these categories; it is never quite so stark as I have declared it; this is purely to illustrate my point. Nevertheless, a dominance shines through in the overall cultural ethos of any organization.

And even within each category, each organization has its distinct personality; its own flavour.

A set of values should be the shorthand for that flavour, within the wider context of its overall characteristics.

So you can observe two different organizations that both have a horizontal culture, but also have two very different sets of values. The cultural model may be the same, but the particular personality differs, according to its business purpose and strategy.

The key point here is that no one culture is right or wrong, better or worse, than any other. It's about . . .

- having the right culture for your organization's conditions, to deliver your strategy

- being committed to putting this culture at the core of your operations

- working hard to ensure how the culture really works and aligns with what you expect.

Culture shouldn't be left to chance and shouldn't be an add-on to 'real business'.

For instance, managers should never take for granted that their expectations are actually happening within the business. It is very unlikely – and very definitely won't be – if they do not consistently and constantly focus on the culture, as they do on strategy and operations.

How on earth could you expect hundreds or thousands of people to consistently act in the way you presume them to, if you have only voiced this expectation once, put it up on a website, or etched it into some glass doors? Culture requires focus and an ongoing maintenance plan. That means forensic inspection as well as planning ahead, in addition to total honesty about the state it is in today.

Culture matters because businesses consist of people, not algorithms (well, for the most part …), and things go wrong or right because of them. Major corporate disasters happen because of human actions, which although sometimes unintentional nonetheless still result in bad outcomes. And on the flip-side, we all know that when a team pulls together, aligns behind a cohesive purpose, clear strategy and consistent ethos, it is one that more often excels.

Businesses are not just a list of tasks to cross off, and while they may seem defined by numbers, they are nothing without people. Which is why this book is vital to understanding your current culture, what it takes to shift it, and how to ensure that shift is lasting.

PART ONE

WHY BOTHER?

This book does not seek to prove why culture is a performance differentiator. As you are reading these words, this book assumes that you already understand this concept. So the focus is instead about how to properly recognise what your culture is, give it due consideration as part of performance, and how to align it to underpin the delivery of your business purpose and strategy.

But to start with a quick recap: this first part outlines some of the reasons cultural alignment is critical for the long-term health of your business, and a real differentiator of performance. It can be your biggest asset or your greatest liability.

That's up to you.

1

The biggest levers

Strategy and culture sit right at the top of the list of levers available to CEOs, to shape performance and ensure the sustainability of the organization. Yet still, too often, while we say that people are the organization's greatest asset, the majority of the leaders' focus, time, effort, brainpower and performance tracking is dedicated to strategy and operations.

Culture, the way that 'greatest asset' behaves, thinks, works, makes decisions, aligns (or doesn't) behind the organization's purpose, is often met with bemused looks. That, or raised eyebrows, sniggers in the corner, outright cynicism, quiet denial, hopeful glances towards HR that they have it covered . . . or any combination of the above.

And in terms of dedicated focus alongside strategy (and operations) in the regular rhythm of the business agenda – well, if it even gets on the agenda, it's probably at the end as a special item, or with a focus on a specific tactical issue, such as the annual engagement survey.

How often does the top team take time to reflect on the culture, deep dive into weak areas, analyse sustainability, and check for emerging risks? It's not unusual to have an annual strategy review, so why do we not have an annual cultural review too?

2

Putting off the inevitable

Culture is a bit like house maintenance; for many of us, until something major goes wrong, you never really worry about it. There may be a few creaks here and there, but you can find workarounds and soldier on as normal. Maybe you have to adopt a few new habits to ensure things keep running ok – an extra push on a stuck door, a bit of masking tape to patch up a hole. And this continues, until something goes wrong that directly and obtrusively impacts daily life; the boiler breaks in the middle of winter, or a massive crack in the walls means huge structural work is required. Suddenly, costs begin to escalate (time and disruption, if not money alone), and we find ourselves asking: Why, oh why, didn't I maintain things properly from the start and avoid all this hassle now?

Getting culture right is exactly like house maintenance: consistently taking time to observe how the organization is working and interacting; looking ahead to what may be needed to help improve it; and keeping a regular schedule of small interventions that support its overall health, in addition to its alignment with what the business needs to deliver. Seeing a problem and just hoping it self-corrects will never work, just as a crack in a wall cannot miraculously close over. It's the same with culture.

You have to watch for the cracks; never ignore them. Better still, with a consistent focus, you can ensure that they do not emerge in the first place.

For instance, the best performing businesses in which people are achieving extraordinary things are:

1   The businesses where people's behaviour and ways of working are aligned and unified behind a stated purpose, a direction and way of doing things – demonstrating shared values.

2   That set of shared values is the demonstrably right set to underpin and reinforce the overall business strategy.

Here, less time is needed for micro-management because employees are clear on how things should be done, and what the priorities are. Vital time can then be funnelled into strategy and innovation, resulting in higher engagement and productivity, with the benefits filtering their way through to customer experience. Employees do not require so many instructions, instead working off core principles that really matter. These core principles are as good as rules but include a greater degree of trust and empowerment – thus eliciting a proportionally greater degree of energy and commitment.

Jørgen Vig Knudstorp – departing LEGO CEO in 2017, commenting on key to LEGO turnaround from 2004 near-bankruptcy

The culture I'm trying to create is one where every year when we celebrate another record result, I get up on the beer box and I say, 'Thank you for doing all of the things I never asked you to do.' I don't want to control. I want to create context. I want to create clarity of culture and strategic choice, but then I want people to surprise me. I don't want a place where people are doing what they've been told to do because that stifles that creative bureaucracy, that creates fear.

And if none of that holds water with you, then just consider how the external context all points to focusing on your culture as a core part of your business, and working it as such.

In other words: soon you won't have a choice but to engage with culture, so why not use this opportunity to get ahead of the pack?

3

Getting your head around it

Focusing on your organization's culture requires tackling how people behave and interact, day in day out. It's more than a theoretical exercise. It's a topic that can be hard to pin a precise value to, and requires something different from a standard project management approach.

It therefore does not come as a surprise that focusing on culture can be seen as either too difficult, too distracting or just too intangible in terms of return.

However, the point is not to be distracted by the nay-sayers, those people in your organization who have all the answers as to why this focus on culture is hocus-pocus (see speech bubbles below).

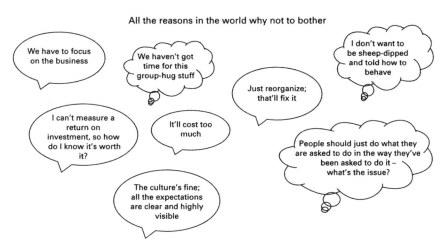

FIGURE 3.1

Now, not everyone will feel this same level of enthusiasm about such work as you do. (In fact, you may be struggling yourself at the start, if someone has tapped you on the shoulder to 'fix it'). There are people who will be dragged along kicking and screaming, and others who will duck their heads whilst quietly hoping it will go away.

So let us assume there are three prime mindsets to tackle here: those who don't want to, those who could be persuaded, and those who consider it a core part of effective business.

i) For those who don't want to: why I have to bother

Regulation

Well, the first thing to note is the ever-increasing regulation, especially in the Western corporate world, putting culture firmly as a core element of business governance and performance. This was given momentum in the years following the global financial crisis, which emerged within the first decade of the twenty-first century.

Some regulation is advisory, but some is also becoming enshrined in law.

UK Financial Reporting Council, Executive Summary of Report on Corporate Culture, July 2016

Key observations

From our discussions with chairmen, chief executives, investors and a broad range of stakeholders and professional organizations we make the following observations about corporate culture:

DEMONSTRATE LEADERSHIP

Leaders, in particular the chief executive, must embody the desired culture, embedding this at all levels and in every aspect of the business. Boards have a responsibility to act where leaders do not deliver.

RECOGNISE THE VALUE OF CULTURE

A healthy corporate culture is a valuable asset, a source of competitive advantage and vital to the creation and protection of long-term value. It is the board's role to determine the purpose of the company and ensure that the company's values, strategy and business model are aligned to it. Directors should not wait for a crisis before they focus on company culture.

BE OPEN AND ACCOUNTABLE

Openness and accountability matter at every level. Good governance means a focus on how this takes place throughout the company and those who act on its behalf. It should be demonstrated in the way the company conducts business and engages with and reports to stakeholders. This involves respecting a wide range of stakeholder interests.

EMBED AND INTEGRATE

The values of the company need to inform the behaviours which are expected of all employees and suppliers. Human resources, internal audit, ethics, compliance, and risk functions should be empowered and resourced to embed values and assess culture effectively. Their voice in the boardroom should be strengthened.

ASSESS, MEASURE AND ENGAGE

Indicators and measures used should be aligned to desired outcomes and material to the business. The board has a responsibility to understand behaviour throughout the company and to challenge where they comprehend misalignment with values or need better information. Boards should devote sufficient resource to evaluating culture and consider how they report on it.

ALIGN VALUES AND INCENTIVES

The performance management and reward system should support and encourage behaviours consistent with the company's purpose, values, strategy and business model. The board is responsible for explaining this alignment clearly to shareholders, employees and other stakeholders.

EXERCISE STEWARDSHIP

Effective stewardship should include engagement about culture and encourage better reporting. Investors should challenge themselves about the behaviours they are encouraging in companies and to reflect on their own culture.

In July 2018 the FRC formalised this guidance through issuing an updated corporate governance code, enshrining the role of the Board and its duties in overseeing an effective corporate culture amongst its other duties and are becoming increasingly vocal in their commentary and censure of companies they believe fall short of the expectations.

Pressure

Investors

Whether it's a large fund or an individual investor looking at an organization's performance, it's not simply the finances they are tracking. Sure, those will be the outcomes they seek and the headlines that catch everyone's eye. But investors tend to dig deeper and wider than that, looking for signals in the system that will give them confidence in plans being met, not just once, but consistently.

With the amount of information accessible from myriad sources, and the instant, global nature of that accessibility, there is no hiding place for an organization; all facets can and will be revealed.

Investment analysts can also significantly influence perceptions. Increasingly, their definitions of performance are broadening from purely financial and operational to encompass social responsibility, organizational health and leading indicators. Their influence on sentiment leads into share price and company valuation.

Crisis

How often does a financial or operational crisis become an investigation into the culture of the organization, the behaviour of and tone from the top, what was being incentivised, the decisions the individuals made? A crisis quickly turns to a cultural navel-gazing, along with all the other root causes the organization examines. Whether you want to tackle culture or not, in this case you will have to.

Societal mood

Public mood can also be hugely impactful. While many stories come and go, momentum can quickly gather around a particular issue. Social media and instant communication means sentiment spreads much faster and louder than it ever has and will continue in that vein. For every company failure in the headlines, scepticism about the culture within large organizations grows.

Whether it's a malaise about corporate life and its culture, or a failure in another part of your sector, you will get dragged into it by association. The moral? Best to have it already covered.

Case Study

Back in the 1990s, the UK began to outsource some of its public services: those activities that could be done more efficiently by private sector companies. This was heralded within the societal mood as progressive, cost-efficient, important for employment growth and so on. Fast forward to 2010–2014 and the mood shifts as companies such as G4S and Serco hit the news around operational challenges in areas such as security and justice. The media furore draws attention to the culture of the leadership and the wider organizations in the services sector. 'Are they just going for profit without a public service ethos?' Fast forward further to 2015–2018 and the profit warnings from Mitie, Interserve, Capita and Carillion, ending in the latter's collapse, and the societal mood starts questioning the structure and workings of the whole contracting and services sector. 'Is the culture of not just the organizations and their leaders, but the boards as well, flawed?' Share prices fall, confidence amongst stakeholders is tentative at best, and Parliamentary Select Committees probe deeply into the culture that is driving risk-taking and decision making. How the mood changes; as it ever will. And mood can turn into operational and financial issues: perception and sentiment can shape the decisions of others. Take a bank, that decides to stop lending to an organization due to the weaker sentiment. When funding dries up, the organization may experience a problem with liquidity.

Mood matters.

Monitors

There are numerous examples of companies that have ethics monitors or culture tsars assigned to them, as part of a post-crisis clean up or conditions alongside a levied fine. You do not have a choice about when they arrive or how long they stay. They will pick apart how you work, who really sets the tone, the cultural expectations formally laid out, and whether they are consistent, communicated, understood and enacted.

Case Study

After the Deepwater Horizon accident in 2010, BP was assigned an 'independent ethics monitor' for a 4-year term by the US government. Their role was to observe and comment on how the company defined its target culture, embedded the culture into its business operations, and tracked how the culture was working on the ground. The remit did not end there: proposals on anything that needed improving were also part of the final report. The Monitor had the remit to go anywhere, ask anything, from anyone, at any time: access all areas, if you like.

ii) For those who could be persuaded: why I might want to bother

It's like Maslow's hierarchy of needs; beyond the 'have to' there is the 'might want to', and the development of a mindset that looks beyond simply managing risk.

Maslow proposed that motivation is the result of a person's attempt at fulfilling five basic needs: physiological, safety, social, esteem and self-actualization. According to Maslow, these needs can create internal pressures that can influence a person's behaviour – and they build from those they 'have to' have, the physiological, to those that are not essential but desirable.

Encouraging people to want to work here

The marketplace for attracting talent is ever more competitive, both because of the way younger generations view companies and careers, and due to the global connected information flow. Potential employee behaviour is discerning. It is decades since talented individuals were attracted en masse to a company because it was the safe option for life; gone are the days when they chose to apply to a company purely on its salary package, benefits and career development. Nowadays we all scrutinise what it is really like to work at a company, how the stated values match up with commentaries about the real working experience, and the way it is conducting business.

You could find yourself pushing water uphill, if what you are espousing is at odds with what people are experiencing, or if nothing stands out in terms of the character and culture of the organization.

Some of the online channels for researching employers, including formal and informal reviews from prospective, current and former employees:

- Glassdoor
- Indeed
- LinkedIn
- Careerbliss

- Twitter
- Facebook
- Google.

The talent currently entering the workforce uses culture as a choice-point for one company over another, and they do their research thoroughly. If they decide that they do not like what they see through their searches, they will find your organization unfavourable. Why? It could be the purpose of the company, the work environment, or it could be any number of elements – but some of the most critically reviewed lie way beyond the salary package.

Don't be the outlier

When a movement of change starts to occur within a specific business issue and leaders take a public stand, it can act as an effective incentive for others to make progress on that topic. Particularly when there is public reporting involved. No one wants to be left behind. Even if it's for reasons of personal reputation, it can spur organizations into action. It is embarrassing, as well as time-consuming, justifying and explaining to all why you are failing to take part along with the others. After all, what does it then say about your culture and character as a company?

Case Study

A prime example of this is the 2011 Davies Report, which challenged FTSE 100 Chairs to reach a goal of at least 25 per cent of board roles being filled by women by 2016.

The starting point was 11 per cent. Reporting occurred every six months, highlighting progress for all to see. 100 companies, just over 1000 roles; a sample size that everyone could work with. Every time the results were published, the group without a single woman on their board became smaller and more loudly called-out. This continued until one was left standing (Glencore): a situation that didn't last long. They appointed a woman to their board in June 2014. By 2016, over 26 per cent of board roles in the FSTE 100 were filled by women. By 2018, with the effort now championed by the Hampton-Alexander remit, progress reached 30 per cent and the focus has extended into the wider FTSE 350 group and with an emphasis on executive roles as well. The same pattern continues. And progress continues to be made – it doesn't always take regulation, peer pressure, and the wrong sort of publicity can instigate action.

Engagement and productivity

Employee surveys can be tick-box exercises; if you choose to treat them that way. But do so at your peril, because these surveys elicit truly valuable insight into how your organization thinks, acts and perceives. Faced with an online questionnaire, more of us will be more honest than sticking our hand up (and our necks out) in a room full of colleagues. As a leader of the organization wondering why productivity is not as high as it could be, or why staff turnover is higher than you'd like, start by taking a look at your employee survey.

Once you have asked their views, and they have supplied you with their insights and opinions, what is the follow up? Not sharing the results, and failing to make any improvements, can have a further detrimental effect. Yet being transparent with the results, seeking out what could help individuals within the organization to want to stay, feel good about their work, and deliver more – well, there's added value to the bottom line when following this approach.

To put it clearly: Be active in finding out what your employee survey says about your culture, share the results with your employees (the good, the bad and the ugly), and then work with them to do something about it.

The fourth industrial age

The era of big data, Internet of Things, Artificial Intelligence, machine learning, neural networking, and numerous other automation systems have enormous implications for the skills required from humans in a working environment. As routine tasks are automated, and the world becomes ever more connected, then relational as well as strategic skills (and that much-used term EQ) become increasingly fundamental and differentiating.

The cultural elements of work become a more pivotal part of our jobs, as repetitive tasks are increasingly conducted by algorithms and machines. These cultural aspects cannot be replicated by bots and so become integral to performance differentiation, as everyone's tasks become equally efficiently delivered by technology.

Case Study

'Whatever the reasons we're fearing for, in terms of machines outrunning us, there isn't one we should actually grieve about. The bots will only deal with all our routine, redundant tasks.

As our future rests in the hands of publicly and privately accessed data, to focus on the actual problems and to make meaningful moves, humans will be wanted to connect the dots creatively. Rather than having to handle tedious workarounds'

Three top skills required in the AI world:

- Sense making
- Social Intelligence
- Adaptive Thinking.

Hackernoon November 2017

---

iii) For those who consider it a core part of effective business: why, of course I'd bother

As there is no need for persuasion here, instead I have provided a few real-life examples of culture impacting business. These are included to reinforce your awareness and develop your knowledge of what eventualities are possible:

Case Studies

Culture (nearly) brings the house down:	Culture and strategy are aligned:
1980s/1990s	
⇨ IBM – from smartest company to a leviathan with a clogged-up culture. It took a radical overhaul, new approach, change of people – and years – to turn its culture around.	⇨ First Direct – a bank that is a consistently superb performer on customer service and stays ahead of other new entrant competitors in the UK. It has no high street presence, purely online and telephone. Values feed through hiring, performance, processes, work environment, to the customer. They drive the performance.

2000s

⇨ Arthur Anderson – surrendered its licence to practice and failed after it emerged that it shredded millions of documents relating to dealings with Enron, which itself had gone bankrupt.

⇨ Lehman Brothers – a 150-year-old firm that gradually turned its culture to one of profit and growth as a purpose. Spectacularly failed, as the global financial crisis hit.

2010s

⇨ Blackberry – it was the prime innovator, then it nearly disappeared as it belatedly realised that its culture was geared toward prioritising the phone over and above the customer, while for Apple and Samsung it was the other way around.

⇨ VW – hugely respected and trusted, until the emissions scandal of 2015 and the realisation of a culture that had allowed this to happen.

⇨ John Lewis & Partners – they are not the cheapest in the retail space, but customer and employee loyalty and trust are maintained through consistent structure and tone of 'partnership'. Their rebranding in Summer 2018 built off and reinforced this culture. Inside and out, their ethos is aligned, structurally, not just behaviourally.

4

All the time, or a moment in time?

So if you are 'bothering' with company culture, when might you need to do so effectively? Does it involve focusing and working upon every day, or is it a one-off effort?

Well, the short answer is: both.

All the time

Firstly, to take us back to the house analogy, focus is required all of the time, but in small doses. In terms of culture, this means constant reviews, checks, looking out for signals to ensure what you have is aligned with what you need; it means making culture a part of your regular agenda, like you would for other parts of performance, whether operational or financial.

Just add in cultural.

It truly is not that hard; rather it is dependent on your will and commitment to carve out the space for it.

Find some measures that act as proxies, telling you whether your organizational culture is on track or it is flickering red lights at you. (Chapter 16:

Filling buckets not spreadsheets in Part Three gives a lot more detail on approaching measurement.)

Flickering red lights: the first signs that your culture needs (more) work

1. Do as I say, not as I do

'What interests the boss, fascinates the team' – if leaders are acting and behaving one way, but the target culture is another, then not only do people notice, they can also become confused from the conflicting signals. If the culture says 'experimentation and innovation', but the leaders are only focused on short term delivery of financial targets, what results may be a very mixed bag. Not to mention how it can breed cynicism about the intentions of the leaders.

---

2. Them and Us

If the leadership of the organization is not accessible, does not reach in to find out people's views or to invite real feedback, then it is similarly unlikely to recognise the real culture that exists. It could be operating with cultural blindness.

---

3. On the shelf

Ask people what the target culture is and what cultural expectations are laid out. If they have to look it up in a book, or refer to a website, or ask a friend, then they are not sufficiently present in the psyche or working practices of the organization.

---

4. Present in body, but not in spirit

Most organizations of a certain size conduct an employee engagement survey on a regular basis, often annually. There could be myriad reasons for why engagement is low, but when it is, it is also a signal that something in the culture isn't working well.

---

5. Nice wallpaper

The purpose, the values, the brand promise: they are all up on the wall, on the desktop screensavers, etched into the glass doors. But if you ask people what really matters within the organization and it doesn't match up with the writing on the walls – then it's simply wallpaper.

---

6. The truth is out there

Don't believe your own hype. Your external stakeholders, whether customers or investors, will have a view on the culture of your organization, formed from how you interact with and appear to them. If they are saying things about your culture because of their experience with you and you don't like what you hear, whether you agree with it or not – you have something to take a look at.

These are simply surface indications that something needs more work. It's important to dig deeper to find out more.

Moments in time

There are moments in time where you will need to direct extra focus and energy into culture work, just like you would for strategy and operations.

These are times of strategic disruption, and you will need to either:

- reflect whether your target culture is still fit for purpose – like a strategy review, or remodelling the house because how you live has changed

  Or

- intervene to bring your current culture in line with your target culture. In effect, you need to fix the hole in the roof first before it rains.

Depending on the context, it may also mean you need to do quite a bit of both.

These moments (of months and years) can then be further split into planned and unplanned disruption:

a) Planned moments

Strategic change: altering the business model, rebranding, USP shift, exiting or entering different markets, and so on.

- Strategy is delivered through culture, through the people in the organization and how they work internally, as well as how they show up to deliver with customers, suppliers and wider stakeholders. So, if something changes in the strategy, it may need to change in the culture. A new geography may require different customer-facing and government practices – an Anglo-Saxon culture may not work well in a Latin American one, for example. Or a new product market may require not just different technical skills, but different cultural ones. For instance, is this about innovation or about smooth operations? Does the current culture encourage experimentation and the associated tolerance of mistakes, and the imperative learning that this necessitates?

Leadership change: new CEO

- The culture of a company should not completely change simply because the most senior leader does, although they certainly have an impact with their tone, style and behaviour. They may decide to take the company in a different direction. In fact, they may have been brought in for that very reason; to make a big change. Often, they bring with them trusted colleagues who will also make an impact.

  Don't walk blindly into this; take stock of the culture today and understand how your new leader's influence aligns or doesn't. It may be that some changes are needed.

Structural change: merger or acquisition integration

- What looked a great deal on paper may turn out to be a huge headache and a serious de-railer, if culture is not focused on as part of the deal, integration and ongoing operation. You wouldn't leave the legal, leadership, IT or financial aspects to change on their own – so why the culture? Companies that simply merge two organizations together and hope that either the lead one subsumes the other's culture, or that together something new and improved will just emerge, leave themselves open to risk of:

  - productivity shortfalls – one group simply doesn't understand the day to day norms in the new structure.

  - loss of talent – rather than losing a sense of identity and place, people leave altogether.

  - bad decisions – without making clear what the new combined culture should be, and working hard towards ensuring that, people may make decisions based on what they think is the right thing but be misinterpreting what is really meant.

b) Unplanned moments

Externally-imposed requirements (as above): regulatory change, external monitor, crisis (reputational, financial or operational)

- Each day, the culture of your organization is within your power to nurture, nudge, adjust. Yet external context often throws curveballs that mean you have no choice but to adapt, whether that means to totally redefine your target culture or to be more actively managing what is already in place. In this situation, you may unconsciously approach it in a heightened state of adrenalin, possibly chaos, certainly stress – and very often faster. Indeed, the context may lend itself to wanting to just 'fix things' as quickly as possible, but these are the times in which it becomes vitally important to work through any issues steadily, and with resilience.

Case Study

In 2017, the extraordinary growth and success of Uber over the previous few years became overshadowed by a crisis. A number of high-profile legal cases around the definition of employment, the suspension of its licence in some cities and various exposés of its culture, created a crisis of reputation. The CEO's behaviour didn't help and even though he was the founder, he was replaced by a new CEO. This 'unplanned moment' drove a re-think of its culture.

On arrival, new CEO Dhara Khosrowshahi had to move fast, and conducted an intense period of listening to employees. Uber's culture, that had been so effective in pushing boundaries and driving growth, had now become a risk rather than an asset and had created this crisis. He asked employees what were the best bits, the bits to drop and the desired culture to go forward. He conducted the exercise across a short time period, only about 3 months.

In November 2017 he announced Uber's new 'cultural norms' saying 'But it's also clear that the culture and approach that got Uber where it is today is not what will get us to the next level. As we move from an era of growth at all costs to one of responsible growth, our culture needs to evolve. Rather than ditching everything, I'm focused on preserving what works while quickly changing what doesn't'.

Over time, the previous Uber management may well have moved to this new culture reflecting its increasing maturity and scale, but the crisis caused a change in leadership and a redefinition at speed, to stabilize the situation.

This is a prime example of culture and strategy moving out of step and creating real problems. As the company grew, it moved from being a disruptive start-up to a monolith, becoming a player amongst the more established organizations, yet its culture and subsequent behaviour continued to manifest as a start-up disruptor. An organization needs to focus on how it does business at different stages of its maturity and scale from a cultural, not simply structural standpoint, and that needs planning.

---

c) Previous lack of attention

Of course it could be that there simply hasn't been a focus on culture before and that the whole topic as something to oversee is a new concept to the leadership. Starting from scratch doesn't have to result from a major upheaval (planned or unplanned), it could be that there is a growing appreciation that to perform into the future, a focus on culture will indeed be required. There is a dawning recognition that to this point, it is simply by luck or goodwill that from a culture perspective things seem to have gone fairly smoothly.

5

Alignment, alignment, alignment – I'll say that again – alignment

With culture it's not about right or wrong, it's about alignment. Never forget this.

I am often asked 'whose culture do you think is the best?'

This is the wrong question.

The real question should be 'who focuses on their culture as a core driver of performance and aligns their culture best with their strategy to deliver what they need?'. (Though I'll admit, it's slightly less punchy).

On its own, with no clear direction to deliver, culture is simply the amassed behaviour of people around a similar core set of values and beliefs. Those beliefs may be the ones stated, or not, depending on the context in which they are operating. Any organization has a culture, whether it is assessed or not, whether it is managed or not, whether it is regarded as a priority in performance or not. From the outside or the inside, traits can be observed that signal 'how things work and get done around here and what really matters'. That's culture as we experience it.

But it needs a purpose, a goal, a direction, to be of real value. If it doesn't have one, it could appear as Brownian motion: lots of energy in a confined space but not achieving anything. Or not achieving what it needs to.

The whole shebang

Organizations consciously line up their strategy with their purpose: the why and the what.

They shift their organizational structure to deliver that strategy: that's some of the how.

But the rest of the 'how' (the culture) is so often left untended. It's in the 'intangible' column for many. And yet, it is the final piece in the jigsaw.

The culture must also line up to ensure the organizational structure works and the strategy can be delivered effectively.

Just putting names and job titles in boxes and changing reporting lines is not on its own going to change how work really gets done to deliver the goals.

The way we interact and make decisions through what we perceive to matter, needs to shift to enable those more formal changes to make the required difference.

Alignment in this case is the whole shebang – the why, the what and the full 'how' of the organization: that includes culture.

The inner workings of culture

Alignment **within** culture is vital. Take a step back and get to grips with what is really making up culture; the dynamics that are driving it. If you can recognise these and accept that they are what they are, whether you like it or not, then you have a better chance at being able to create the culture you need.

Any culture has two aspects:

- Formal – the expectations that are laid out publicly, they are the ones that are hosted on the company website, quite often underneath a section titled 'Who we are'

- Informal – the practices, networks, influences, perceptions, decision making approach that sums up how work gets done . . . really.

Too often, organizations focus on the formal, either hoping the informal will just go away or die quietly if the formal expectations are expressed more vocally, more often and perhaps with the occasional campaign and incentive. Shout louder till you hear me.

It's not so straightforward. Human beings are involved, and we don't all think alike; we don't all act alike. Thank goodness.

We are adults exercising our own free will, so we choose how best to get things done and we make our own minds up about what really matters; then act accordingly. That's not to say we maliciously act against the formal expectations, but just that they may sometimes seem weak, remote, not applicable or highly transient. If that is topped off with no one stopping me from working and behaving the way I do today, and if there is nothing in it for me to work differently, then I am just as likely to carry on as I have been, as I am to shift my patterns of behaviour and decision making. In fact, your own status quo is more likely.

So, what is happening day in, day out, when no one is looking (the informal), cannot be ignored. Don't bury your head in the sand like an ostrich and hope to goodness the formal expectations are simply how it is. If you are not overseeing it like you are doing with strategy or organizational structure, then the chances are your informal will not only be different from your expectations, it could be working against it, or at the very least, around it. And that isn't just others; that's more than likely also you and at the very least, much of the senior leadership. The more senior you are, the bigger that impact is on the wider organization. What you say you want, and what you do, in terms of behaviours, aren't just for others; it's for everyone in the organization.

Alignment is for everyone.

I view the formal expectations as the Strategic part of culture, while the informal parts consist of a mixture of Social and Political.

- Strategic – stated expectations. The words that are communicated and repeated through official channels. You'll see them on the website, in the annual report. Our Values, Who we are, Our Culture. All stakeholders see these expectations: they are the label on the tin of the organization.

- Social – common practices, networks, communities, peer groups. Every day, we get things done in the way we find most efficient and that can be on our own or through other people. We have our daily habits, the people we are used to working with, the ones we seek advice from, the groups that provide us with a sense of belonging, or agree on a particular way of viewing things. All of this is our modus operandi, whether it is conscious or subconscious. It's just the way we operate.

- Political – who or what influences decisions, where and when decisions are made and by whom, how this is perceived, what is understood to really matter. How much is done by consensus, does external reputation influence the big decisions or does the organization stay the course, are decisions made in a meeting or before, or even are they changed afterwards? Do people end up second-guessing what might be decided differently even though a decision or direction has been already communicated? How transparent is the decision making and influence process?

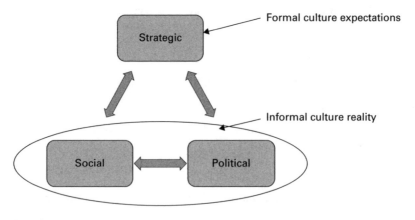

FIGURE 5.1

No matter whether you need to redefine your cultural expectations or not, aligning the informal with the formal is vital for being able to drive your culture to underpin your organizational structure and align to deliver your strategy.

If your expectations are appropriate and the social parts of your culture are operating in line with them, but behind the scenes people are taking different sorts of decisions, eventually the social aspect will adjust how it operates as it observes and experiences 'what really matters around here'.

If your political situation is becoming toxic, then you may find the social side of the organization hunkers down and tries to get on with what needs to be done, riding out what it sees as a distraction at decision-making levels. It may end up as a 'we've been here before and seen it all before' culture, which then becomes really difficult to bring back from cynicism.

Either way, pay attention to what is going on in the informal organization and work to align both parts of it together, and with the formal expectations.

When the different aspects of culture are out of line for any length of time, it can lead to disfunction or worse, unpredictability, at the very moments when things get difficult and you need consistency.

As well as providing you with an approach to defining the culture you need, this book goes into some detail about how to ensure that your informal culture lines up with those formal expectations you may have spent so long drawing out.

6

Sorry, what's the question again?

Remember, to start effectively shifting the culture, you need to know what needs shifting:

- Is the case simply that the way things are working today is not what you've been asking for? Is there a misalignment between what the CEO asks for and how it really works when they're not in the room? (Social and Political don't align with Strategic.)

  Or

- Is what you've been asking for not what you really need for your business to be successful? You may have great alignment between what the CEO asks for and how it works when they are not in the room; but its remains a culture that continues to fail in helping the business deliver against its purpose and strategy. Do you in fact need to redefine the target culture?

  Or (in very many cases)

- A bit of both.

Make sure to not get fixated purely on changing the target culture; always acknowledge the distinction between the two elements. You may not need to change what you expect, but you may well need to change what you actually have.

One focus is aligning what is really going on with how you want it to be. The other is to make sure that how you want it to be is actually going to support your business to succeed.

It may be that you are asking one of these questions, yet more often than not, the second question is the one that people start with: Is the culture I have laid out the one I need to win in my business?

Due to a planned or unplanned disruption, you may be prompted to take a look at the culture you need, and then have to step back and reflect on what you actually have today.

Peeling back the layers of the onion if you like.

Of course, the smart thing to do would be to have a constant focus on your culture (the 'all of the time' approach), as this way you are more likely to know what you already have when the disruption comes along. Then all you need to do is focus on checking what you really need and making the shift from there.

But we live in the real world. Let's face it, like house maintenance we mostly only have a big reflection and re-planning session when something goes wrong, when we are forced to take a closer, harder look.

PART TWO

SETTING IT UP

7

Vital ingredients

To do this properly, it will feel like a huge amount of thinking, planning, reflecting, and quite frankly, navel-gazing, before you really get going. But the navel-gazing is very much part of getting going.

In fact, if you dive right in without doing it, you are falling into the first trap around organizational culture: that being active, doing tasks, fixing problems – going at it hell for leather – are all the way to get things moving in the right direction.

Wrong.

Even if you're now crystal clear that you need to do some of this work all of the time as part of the regular business rhythm and some of this work as part of disruption, just hold back a minute more (or maybe a few months more . . .).

While of course if you are the CEO, then you are the ultimate sponsor of the work, and the true 'owner' (just like for strategy); but you can't be actively coordinating and overseeing it on a daily basis. Someone needs to be dedicated to this.

Who is the right person to lead the work? What traits do they need, what experience should they have, what relationship do they have with the top team and where should they best sit to be as effective as possible? Are they known around the wider organization, and are they trusted? What signal does their appointment send out across the organization?

And what about the people who have asked for the work to be done; the very top team? Where are their heads and energy on this?

If you are the CEO, never assume that simply because you have commissioned this focus on culture that the whole of your team has the same enthusiasm or mindset about the work. Has this been something you've discussed together or purely your decision? Is the team supportive, do they view it as an important piece of work: do they get it? If you are not the CEO, keep that firmly in mind – never assume.

Given how notoriously controversial, misunderstood or avoided this sort of work is, these two considerations are vital:

- Who should lead this work?
- How aligned and supportive is the top team?

Who should lead this work?

To answer that, we need to split this into three questions:

1 What experience does the individual have?
2 Where in the organization should this work be led from?
3 What traits are required to do this sort of work?

Having done this work a number of times, whether leading it myself or advising others, on every occasion, the starting assumption or position has been:

- Middle management
- With an HR or Communications background (possibly marketing and brand)
- Energy and passion for this sort of work.

Only one of those three is what I'd advocate – energy and passion for this sort of work. More of that in the section on traits, below.

The person leading this work, or tasked with being the focal point day in day out, needs to have the authority to be able to talk on behalf of the whole company in this area, be able to have trusted, challenging and very honest conversations with the most senior leadership. A useful analogy is to think of this person as having the calibre and standing of an individual leading the strategy work for the organization. Don't settle for less.

There is also a considerable amount of theatre in the appointment and positioning of this role, as it sends a signal on how core this is to overall performance.

This is not a consideration to be taken likely. Any organization should be thoughtful and deliberate in your decision-making for this role.

1. What experience does the individual have?

In this instance, the experience I'm referring to may be surprising. It doesn't need to come from a particular job family. Instead, the ideal mix involves four elements:

- Legacy
- Operational relevance
- Skin in the game
- Traction.

This mix has as much to do with the perception it breeds in others of the work being core and critical, as it does with how it equips you to do the role.

Legacy

Understanding the culture today takes more than a superficial glance. What may seem either obvious or illogical may have very different roots to what's initially perceived. Making sense of today's culture and how to use it to move things forward, benefits from someone having a good grasp on the nuances and some of the long-held myths and stories. That means they need a history within the organization; ideally a good few years. It's not an easy mix to find – someone who has been around a while, but who can still stand back, recognise and call out what's going on – but it is an element of experience that can make all the difference to the work having an impact. Being a critical friend is vital and doing that from 'the inside' can have more impact.

Operational relevance

For culture work to take hold and a shift or adjustment to really happen, the person leading it has to be able to get the ear of the operational areas – the front line. Those colleagues must believe that person will indeed listen to them, share ideas up the line, feedback updates, and be honest, not resorting to spin. Having experience in these sorts of roles, whether as a supervisor or a team member, can make all the difference in accessing the real views and ideas from the mass of colleagues in any organization.

Skin in the game

This person needs to be going places. Whether they are on a fast track as a high flyer, or whether they are already operating at a senior level (no less senior than CEO-2) it's important they are regarded as having a stake in the future of the organization and someone who has skin in the game from their own career perspective. If this work really matters to the overall performance of the organization, then the person leading it should represent that.

Traction

The preceding three elements of experience, while vital, will be limited in their value if the relationship that person holds with the most senior team is flawed.

Shifting a culture relies in the first instance on the very top team being able to look in the mirror, and that must be facilitated by someone they are comfortable around and that they trust to keep things confidential; or they just won't open up.

2. Where in the organization should this work be led from?

The common assumption is to position culture work within one of the people functions, because it's all about engagement and behaviour. Typical locations are within Human Resources, notably learning, development, inclusion, leadership or talent (or any combination thereof) and Communications. However, this sends exactly the signal to the sceptics that you are trying to overcome – that this is separate from day to day business operations and not at the core of hard-edged business performance. Also watch out for those wanting to position the work reporting into Marketing – this isn't brand. Yes, your brand will be reinforced if your culture internally is lined up with it and operating well, but your culture is first and foremost about how you interact, behave and make business decisions as an organization, across the whole set of activities, not just in facing out to your customers and other stakeholders.

As with the experience required for the role, perception of the positioning of this work is as important as its organizational location and that means consciously placing it in an indisputably neutral and yet core, situation in the organizational structure.

While reporting the role directly into the CEO is ideal, this isn't always practical. Second best is reporting into the Chief Operating Officer or Chief of Staff. I have also seen it reported into the Group Risk Officer; though while this fulfils many of the criteria, it can leave it perceived as only managing the downside, and not an opportunity for productivity improvements.

3. What traits are required to do this sort of work?

This work isn't for everyone; if you thrive in situations where certainty is all, activity is managed to precise deadlines and return on investment is clear and tangible, then look away now.

If, however, you are looking for a challenge where you orchestrate a system shift, work through influence, adjust your activity according to the traction within the organization, use carrot and stick to move things forward (and using that stick is essential sometimes) all within the boundaries of a clear, unshifting goal that takes years to achieve; then this is the role for you.

It sounds like a fairly masochistic role on the surface, and in some ways, it is just that. Your role is to enrol, engage and equip the organization to shift the system, not for you to be doing it yourself. In that respect, the best outcomes can be represented by an organization who believes 'it's just happened over time'. In this role, if you have done your job well, don't expect the organization to see you as the hero of the hour. You will have to receive your thanks and rewards purely from those you report to.

Extraversion or introversion are not the important distinctions in such a role. But a heady cocktail of seemingly disparate traits, do, in my experience, provide the mix of qualities that are essential to you being effective.

There are six of them:

- Passion
- Perception
- Patience
- Pedantry
- Pragmatism
- Pig-headedness.

Passion

Leading this sort of work can be frustrating and feel like pushing water uphill. After all, the objective is to shift a system such that the way people interact, behave and make decisions changes to line up with a specific set of expectations. It's never going to be straightforward, and simply 'pulling levers' won't bring sustained progress.

At the same time, it is phenomenally rewarding for the individual who has the curiosity and energy to understand what makes people tick, to act as a conduit between the wider organization and the most senior leadership, to find a way to create a lasting shift in the way an organization carries out its purpose.

They will need to be omnipresent in terms of accessibility through all channels for colleagues, so they can be in contact with them whenever and however they want. That doesn't mean all face to face, it will very often be via all the other channels – audio, video, email, text, internal social media and so on. They must have their eyes and ears open using all tools available to them, to ensure they have a good feel for the pulse and temperature check of the culture at any time.

Not only do they need bundles of energy for this work to be so 'available' but they are highly visible: the beacon, the focus, the brand of this culture work. Colleagues are watching for signals that this work is really important or whether it is just another flash in the pan. Their passion for it, consistently, is one of those signals. For some, this work is a leap of faith, so the ability to provide belief that it will make a difference and that the organization will see it through, is key.

Perception

Emotional intelligence, EQ, mindfulness, self-awareness, listening to your gut, catching yourself on (as my Mother would say) – any and all of these are required here. Whatever labels you choose to put on it, perception is vital. This work cannot be moved forward or measured on tangible data alone. A healthy dose of the good old-fashioned 'sniff test' is crucial when leading culture work.

It is as much about what is not said and what is not done, as it is about what happens proactively. Noticing patterns in behaviour, digging beneath words spoken to understand meaning, recognising meaning in body language: these are all pieces of data. In fact, in an initial assessment of a situation, much as one should never leap to conclusions, using exactly these sorts of data can be essential to get a first sense of what is going on.

Case Study

I was visiting an operational site at a company recently. I drove into the car park and spotted the visitors' parking spaces. The spaces were marked with signs showing two company brands side by side. All very well, since the work had been being carried out by both companies in a 50:50 joint venture. But not anymore; in fact, not for the last six months since this company had taken over 100% of the contract. My very first reaction was that something wasn't going to be right about the culture of the organization doing this work if the leadership had not paid enough attention to update such a visible sign of identity – in six months. This wasn't about brand, this was about the finer details of the leadership focus. It was only one signal, but I had a hunch. Indeed it turned out to be a very telling signal; I experienced a culture that was not working very well as a result of a leadership that had not purposefully integrated the two previous cultures into one. There was inefficiency, a lack of energy and focus, and the overall performance of the operation was not as it should have been. When I reported back to the leadership, it emerged that the key client had also noticed a drop in operational standards. This was impacting performance. It only took a sign in a car park to send the wrong signal to me, but it was the surface of something deeper.

Look out for the small stuff; it is often an indicator of something much bigger.

Don't assume perception is purely for looking outwards. The person leading this work must be sure to turn the mirror on themselves regularly; to step back and think how they are showing up. Others will be reading much into the signals they are sending. Given it is work that many will be unfamiliar with, some will be sceptical about, they act as a beacon that signals how others should consider the work. They must think about the situation they are in or going into and adjust their demeanour and focus accordingly.

Patience

Quick wins are great, and they should be celebrated to give people a sense of belief that things are moving in the right direction, that what they are doing is making a difference, that the work is under way. But the change leader here mustn't fooled by seeing one good example of the culture in action, that the system has changed and that everything is now aligned. They have to ask themselves, if the push on this work disappeared tomorrow, how much of this culture we're trying to inculcate, would remain, or how quickly would it go back to how it was?

The patience required is to look for signals that the system in which everyone is operating, is really shifting to reinforce, as well as reflect, the target culture.

It's encouraging to see people add the organization's values to their email signatures, but that doesn't yet signal a change in behaviour or that business decisions are being guided by what's expected culturally. It is a positive sign of awareness and engagement but it's simply that. It must be encouraged, recognised, celebrated, but there shouldn't be complacency that much has changed – yet.

The patience required may be more like years than months.

Case Study

Take the example of a company that embedded its refreshed cultural expectations into its performance management process. On the surface, what an excellent sign of the system lining up to reinforce the culture expected. In theory, yes; but in reality, in the first year, many people chose to rate performance versus behaviours that they thought were important, not the ones the company had laid out. In the second year, a drop-down menu on the online form made sure that everyone could only pick the company behaviours to rate against. It wasn't until the third year that individuals were ranked up or down versus others not just on achievement of their objectives but for the behaviours they'd displayed in the way they delivered them. If victory had been declared after the first year, all that would have been achieved was a theoretical sense that behaviours (whoever's) were now part of the form to fill in.

Patience – required.

Pedantry

Being a stickler for the detail is not perhaps the first trait that springs to mind, when Perception and Passion are in such demand. But the finer details really matter here, and the person leading this work must have both the grit and the support to ensure it is maintained.

The cultural expectations, the specifics of the culture lead's remit, the language used to describe the work; these, and many other areas, are micro-elements that reinforce or detract from the system really shifting.

Case Study

Take the cultural expectations. If you haven't been the final decision maker, if you don't really want to change, then it's much simpler to simply interpret things for your own context, change them a bit, fudge it a bit, and carry on as before. This is just another initiative isn't it? It too will pass. After we had defined the refreshed cultural expectations, and particularly the values and behaviours at BP in 2011, when it came to applying them several people wanted to change the wording slightly for their own team. Their view was that it didn't quite fit them and their context. And therein lies a problem – unless it is clear for all, and followed through, that these are the expectations and they don't change, a jot, then within a year, there is a chance there would be myriad versions in operation and no common understanding of the meaning.

Needless to say, I didn't allow it. And behind the scenes I had made sure I had the backing of the CEO and his team to make that decision. Inconsistency at the outset, averted.

You will find many of these examples referred to throughout the ensuing chapters.

The person leading this work needs to have verve in driving precision where it matters.

Pragmatism

Of course, they need to have a clear goal and yes, a plan in terms of approach. They'll need to know what the overall success factors look like, how to track progress, what tools to use and people to partner with. But it's not about having swim-lanes of activity and deadlines on an Excel spreadsheet and then deciding whether things are off-track because the activity hasn't happened on time. This work is not about holding to a plan that is on-track because of a number of meetings that have taken place, or the numbers of people who have volunteered for a network to make change. These are all the activities the coordinator of this work is putting into the system: whether a plan is on- or off-track depends on whether the defined success factors are making progress.

Nor is it about sticking to the plan or tools because of stated intentions. That Perception trait must be used in concert with Pragmatism. Adaptability, being decisive, not being a slave to their own great idea are all important here. Can this person look out for what people are hooked by, where the traction is and then adjust to do more of that? If something they thought was really engaging just isn't grabbing people's attention, then they shouldn't waste energy trying to persuade people why it should; they should cut it and do more of the thing that is working.

Knowing where the pedantry needs to stop and pragmatism needs to take over, is a skill in itself. These traits don't always sit easily as bedfellows. Like a system of organizational values, they can be in healthy tension. It's the balance of them all that needs to be in play.

Case Study

When we finalised the updated purpose and values statements at BP and engagement was building across the organization, we had held to quite some pedantry (as above) around the words. And we didn't stop at just the words; we wanted to ensure the format was consistently applied so that people would recognise the words when they saw them. This came down to the font, the colour and even to the order in which the values were presented. We had agreed that thousands of people being able to reel off the five values in the same order was part of our efforts to ensure consistency, familiarity and awareness.

A few months later I visited one of the company's chemical plants in the US where they were extremely proud of the work they had been doing to embrace the values, bring them to life, and to embed them in their processes. They had invited me to take a look, as they believed they were one of the exemplar parts of the business in their approach to this. Indeed they were. But my first thought was; 'they have the order wrong on the values. I don't care that their order spells out a word, it needs to be as per the order from the company HQ'. Luckily, for once, I didn't say anything at the time; but as I was working out, back in the UK, how to speak to the site manager to adjust all his local engagement materials, one of my team took me aside and helped me see that this would have been purist nonsense. They were engaged, energetic and focused about using the values. If it worked for them to remember them in a different order, it didn't actually make any difference to how they were applying them. So I didn't say anything. They were an exemplar, and they remained so. Having an operational site manager energised about the culture work and on loud-speaker about how they were making a difference to his business, was infinitesimally more valuable than getting the order of the words locally to fit with the order centrally.

Pig-headedness

There is a certain belligerence required for this work; not just in setting it up well, but seeing it through. Many will want to declare victory too early, many more will just want this 'culture initiative done so we can get back to business', and a significant percentage will just get a bit bored with it.

It will be important to keep reiterating the importance of performance to this work, reminding of the overall goal and time expectations laid out at the start, as well as how progress is being tracked. Passion must be on display even if, as the leader of the work, at that moment, it doesn't feel like there is much left. And if it takes a bit of a 'losing it' moment with those in influence, then it may just be called for (in very rare circumstances) to remind the ultimate decision makers what they signed-up for. They shouldn't be swayed, or sidetracked to look at other projects; keeping focused on this work. This goes hand in hand with Patience; being clear from the start that this will take up to three annual cycles to really see a marked shift. They may receive plenty of support at the start of the work for that, but along the way, arguments about changing context, new priorities and 'don't you want a new challenge' will inevitably land at their door. They need to be resilient to resist. Pig-headed, in fact.

Finding the right balance between being firm, focused and determined and being seen to be obstinate and out of touch, is not easy. Each context will be its own, with different players, markets, drivers for the work, but a resilience to hold the line when others wobble, is as much a required trait as the previous five.

Case Study

Even after being asked to lead the work at BP by the CEO, there was the challenge of gaining support for exactly how I was going to lead and approach it. The assumption had been that I would source resource from the external consultants running the overall change programme office, with the usual focus of central control and activity planning. I had to be extremely pig-headed with a couple of senior leaders who were somewhat dismissive of the ability to deliver what we needed, using my approach of internal resources (and hardly any of them) and an air-traffic control philosophy. Of course, the passion I had for the work and the long term working relationship I had with other senior leaders in the firm all mattered. But suddenly everyone above me became an expert overnight on how to do this sort of work. I would have faltered and probably gone for the 'easy life' of accepted practice about how change could occur and the limitations of what we might achieve if I hadn't learned what worked and what didn't from my previous (failed) efforts. I stood firm, refused to budge, and cracked on. Not easy, and credit to those who went with me. But it was a real deep-breath moment with a few comments such as 'you'll never pull this off' actually spurring me on. Perhaps they knew what they were doing and using reverse psychology. If that was the case, I fell for it.

This is not for the faint-hearted.

How aligned and supportive is the top team?

Part One outlined some of the reasons this sort of work is started (disruption, planned or unplanned), and that can influence how the CEO and the top team approach this and their attitude towards it.

While there is no point in doing this work if the CEO is not behind it, it doesn't solely rest with that person's support and drive. The commitment of the rest of the team makes a huge difference too.

If you are not the CEO and have been asked to lead this work, you will need to get the measure of what they are wanting to achieve and how they plan to be involved.

Go into this with your eyes wide open and spend some real time upfront with them to understand their drive. Don't assume you know. Are they driven by a change in strategy and trying to ensure the culture underpins that, are they driven by an impending sense of crisis, do they see this as an opportunity or simply managing some downside risk, or is this a natural evolution of the organization's maturity? Do they even have a clear view themselves? It's not that you need to make a big plan out of this mindset, it's just important to know where the CEO's head and motivation is. You are, after all, acting as their agent, to shift the system.

If you are the CEO, then be proactive and share all this with the person you have appointed. Make the time.

While the CEO lays out the expectation for the work to be done and the right person may be in place to lead the work, it's naïvely heroic to think two people can work on their own without a broader coalition at the most senior levels.

Understanding the mindset of the CEO's immediate team is therefore another key ingredient as you set up the work.

In this respect, I am referring to mindset as the level of commitment to the work on culture in the first place, not on the specifics of the culture itself. (See Part Three, Chapter 11 for digging more deeply into recognising where the culture is today and where it needs to be.)

What is the balance across the team between those who are:

- proactively supportive of purposefully focusing on the culture to underpin strategy;

- passively observing the work is about to begin but waiting on others to show support before they provide the vocal and active commitment;

- silently regarding this as a distraction (see Chapter 1).

It's risky to assume you know where everyone sits.

Typically, there is a split of one third, one third and one third in any team faced with any change; but that will depend on current context, tenure and background of the individuals, and a wealth of other factors that mean this is not a standard answer. Whether you are the CEO or the person chosen to lead the work day to day, do your homework, so you are aware of how the land lies beyond that CEO role. Don't be naïve that it won't matter – it will.

And if absolutely necessary, call it.

Moving forward enthusiastically while simply hoping that enough of the top team are on board to support and reinforce the work, is folly. It will come back to bite you soon; more often sooner rather than later, as you find roadblocks wherever you head.

It does not need the whole team to be proactively supportive. In my experience, three to four in any ten being committed and focused, is practical and realistic.

Case Study

I tried to get the work going twice before in BP; but I had relied on hope and optimism too much in earlier efforts, which were also in very different contexts. I had assumed that because the CEO had asked me to do the work, 1) They were clear why it was needed and what they wanted to achieve, and 2) The whole of their team was on-board. I was naïve. I didn't dig deep enough or ask enough questions and frankly was too excited to see the work finally being set in motion and to have the chance to lead the work in the first place to face the reality of where the mindset really was. Subconsciously I was holding myself back from really probing this as I was concerned I wouldn't like the answer – which was really that there wasn't alignment as to what this would take. It came back to bite – both times the work got so far, and stalled. I should have called it, earlier.

Ask, in one-to-one meetings 'what's your view on doing this work and what do you think it will take to make it matter?' or 'what's your advice on the best way to do this work?' It will be very telling how each of them answers the question.

And remember, once you have sized up where the commitment and alignment is amongst the top team, it's the role of the CEO to call it back out and to signal personal support for the work, and what it's going to take.

Case Study – CEO to the rescue

A couple of months into the work at BP, I held an offsite meeting with the top team to try something a bit different as we really needed to work on some fundamental elements around ambition. I opened up the day and asked for views in the room, fears, concerns, hopes for the session.

A couple of people started out with standard comments around objectives for the session, then another took a deep breath and shared why they believed now was not the right time to do the work this way, that there were other priorities and that this was really taking too much time.

It was one of those moments that feels as if a stone has dropped to the pit of your stomach. I waited, and waited, and there was silence. That's it, I thought. End of. Here we go again.

But no, the CEO stepped in, very calmly, and reminded the team that while this was a difficult time and it might feel as if there are other priorities, creating clarity for all across the company was essential and it had to start in the top team. The work would continue, we would all feel rather uncomfortable, but we had to push on, and be honest with ourselves.

The discussions I'd had right up front with the CEO and then his signalling to the team to empathise with them that he understood not everyone was fully comfortable, made the difference.

Case Studies – senior team enrolment

a) Making the linkage between culture and performance

I was asked to help a FTSE 100 company build a more cohesive culture to enable better performance. Part of this work involved helping them define and embed a single set of company values, from the several sets already in existence as a result of its various brands. I knew the CEO was passionate about this work. He regarded a set of values as the shorthand for the target culture required to deliver the company's strategy and purpose. And I knew he was willing to put in the time and effort to do this properly. But I wasn't sure where the rest of his team really sat on this topic. There was plenty of verbal support in the first team meetings on the subject, but I only really understood where both the appetite and the commitment lay once I interviewed each one of them on their own. I didn't ask the question directly ('do you think this work is important', 'how do you think this will make a difference to performance') – I asked them where they wanted to move the culture to, what was missing in performance today and why, and waited to see who made the linkages between those three areas. Once I'd done that, I had a much better idea of the starting point around values and performance. As with so many teams, 1/3 made the linkage between values (culture) and performance, 1/3 didn't, 1/3 could see a linkage in theory but didn't think it was that critical overall. At least I knew from the start where their collective headspace was, given the individual positions and where I'd therefore need to work hardest.

b) Change appetite

An international financial services organization that had spent the previous few years in recovery mode, asked me to help them analyse whether their current culture was fit to drive growth. It soon became clear that what had worked for recovery was going to need a few adjustments. As it was, it wasn't going to fuel growth. It was by no means broken, it didn't need a big rewrite of its values. If lived out, they certainly could drive growth. But people were not clear what winning really looked like: what was the strategy, where was the goal, other than 'growth' where were they heading? A first task of the leadership team was agreed to be defining that goal, not just in numbers, but also in culture – the balanced scorecard of winning. The team split into two groups to spend two hours drafting the goal up.

What happened was quite revealing.

One group focused on the content of the goal as asked – the numbers, the culture, the boundaries within which it would happen, the timeline. The other group spent the full two hours debating issues around dress code, office tidiness and how purpose, vision, strategy, values and behaviours hung together as a framework. This exercise alone showed me where the change appetite sat across the whole team: certainly not in the second group.

Again, understanding where the leadership headspace is at the start of the work provides you with vital data on where to focus and what, or who, to watch out for.

It's valuable to have a sense across the entire organization of this balance; but it doesn't need to be quite as specifically defined as within the top team, where the numbers are smaller but the individual influence is so much more acute. This is about setting it up to be able to get moving. There is a long way ahead, including constantly checking the temperature of the organization, but that doesn't need to be completely pinned down just yet.

It may seem counter-intuitive, but the group in the middle (who may be passive or slightly sceptical about the work) are the ones that really need focus, so it's worth getting some sense of where those mindsets sit across the organization. Those who are supportive and already engaged just need nudging in the right direction and consistent support. Those who are extremely negative may never take part. I'm not advocating ignoring them or their impact, but it may be diminishing marginal returns in terms of effort-in for shift-out.

There's much more on who to work with and how in Part Three: The Hard Yards, Chapter 14: Shape-shifting and the life of a chameleon.

At a glance

The most impactful leaders of this work have a mix of:

- Legacy
- Operational relevance
- Skin in the game
- Traction.

Where that leader reports into sends a signal:

- Preferably to CEO, COO, Chief of Staff
- Don't default to 'HR owns it'; it doesn't, any more than anyone else.

They need to be able to balance these six traits to thrive in this work: it's not for everyone:

- Passion
- Perception
- Patience
- Pragmatism
- Pedantry
- Pig-headedness.

CEO's motivation and goals for the work need to be clear and understood.

Never assume the top team is all equally supportive or committed about it:

- Be practical – not everyone will be on side, but three out of ten starts to make a difference.

Follow 1/3, 1/3, 1/3 rule and work out who's where: top team and across the organization:

- The passive or slightly sceptical middle is where to really focus.

8

Stopping before starting

Whether you are the CEO, the person asked to lead this work, or a critical function such as HR, taking the time to be clear what it is you're doing, what you aren't doing, and how you're going to go about it, before you start, is essential. Jump in without considering, and confusion will eventually reign, and steps will have to be retraced. Everyone will have different views of what the role of the culture lead is and what the remit is. They will also have differing ideas on how decisions will be made, by whom and when, and how the role will really play out in practice.

Never assume even the key decision makers are all clear: it is highly unlikely that they will be. It's important the most senior stakeholders and the culture lead are aligned. Take the time up front; it may well feel like wheel-spinning, but it is essential to instil momentum further down the line. This could take anything from a few days, to a couple of months. Don't rush through it just to 'get started': taking the time upfront is indeed starting . . . properly.

If you are the person who has been asked to lead this work, stop before you start: consider your role, your remit, what it is you're producing, how big decisions will be made, the process itself of change and how the work will get done. Otherwise you could well end up amongst the pelicans in Finding Nemo with everyone shouting 'Mine, Mine, Mine!!!' Worse still, you could end up at the opposite end of the spectrum with all fingers pointing at you as everyone abrogates all responsibility and declares it's you who is tasked with delivering the culture and any shift required.

It isn't; and it can't be. Culture, whether undergoing a big shift, or simply ongoing focus to ensure alignment, is everyone's responsibility, and everyone impacts it. You are the air-traffic controller. But it's vital for all to understand the rules and the space in which you are operating, and where you are not.

Resist diving in until you are clear.

Terms of reference

There are two clear questions that the senior team needs to address before anyone moves into action mode:

- Is there a clear and common view of the problem to be solved and thereby what needs to be achieved?
- Is there a clear and common view of the culture lead role?

It's too often true that the answers to both of these questions are very unlikely to be yes, in the first instance. In fact, it's unlikely to be yes to either of them. More likely, everyone will believe everyone is in agreement and alignment – but they are not. Which is why it is critical to have the conversation about what it seems to be. The culture lead will have (or should have) their own view as well as the senior team, which should be articulated simply and clearly; though held sufficiently lightly such to be open to improvements given the views from others.

Too often we dive into any piece of work without stepping back and being really clear what the real remit is. And we label others as 'wrong' if they don't agree with our first declaration.

The culture lead should ask the questions of the CEO first, to establish whether the two of them are in the same place or not. Then the direct reports should be asked, as well as a few peers and confidantes. It's always valuable to get a 360-degree view of initial assumptions. It can be quite a useful proxy for what problem people want solved.

Each element should be unpicked. As per the traits required for this role outlined in 'Chapter 7: Vital ingredients', this may show up as pedantry; and that's ok, because so many efforts around organizational culture ultimately have limited impact because they've rushed to action before considering whether everyone is clear on the what and the how.

The problem to be solved and what needs to be achieved

- Is it believed that the expected culture is not the right one to deliver the strategy?

- Is the issue that the expected culture and the current culture aren't the same thing?

- Might some believe that culture is not regarded as important and that more focus is required?

- Is the expected culture appropriate but everything needs a little dialling up – it's all a bit too passive?

- Some or all of the above?

Once there is a shared sense of where the problem really lies, then it'll become clearer what needs to be produced (if anything). Is there a new meaningful mantra required for the organization, is it about following an existing one better, or is it a complete overhaul of what the company is really about?

At this stage, there may be some data, but the exact scale of the issue and the task ahead is very much a judgement. Without delving into a real understanding of today's culture, tomorrow's requirements and where the different stakeholders in and out of the organization perceive the situation, you are still in 'broad brush' territory. Yet it is still very important to have the conversation of these areas at the start to at least define what the nature of the issue is.

The culture lead's role

Be thoughtful about the title of the role. Language can be significant: Culture Change Project Manager provides a different signal to the organization than Culture Integration Lead, or Chief Culture Officer. Think critically about this and only agree the title once the remit of the role is really clear and ironed out between the CEO, top team and the person who is taking the role.

If you are the person taking the role, you will no doubt hear 'you are in charge of Culture'. It's open to vast amounts of interpretation, misrepresentation and assumption. And it's inaccurate: everyone is in charge of culture as it's the total sum of all our behaviours and perceptions and we all impact it. But more of that later.

Case Study

In my work at BP, it took three months to be absolutely specific on what was and wasn't in the remit of 'sorting the culture out'. Taking three months to write what amounted to three sentences may sound unnecessarily picky, but that's what happened, and in retrospect, the discussions and redrafts were time well spent or we would have set off with very different assumptions about the work ahead.

We were all in alignment that, with a sense that the organization was operating to too many assumed sets of cultural expectations, a redefining of the target culture via a purpose statement and a set of values was required. But there were varying different views of whether it was redefining what was expected of leadership or whether it was expected behaviours for all that needed to be re-set.

After a number of discussions, we agreed on behaviours for all – a redefinition of anything additional and specific for leadership could come later, after the behaviours had become part of the 'new normal'. We then needed to align around what was in my remit and what wasn't. Sounds simple; but not so.

My role was Group Head of Organizational Effectiveness; summing up the overall goal of all the work I was leading. Within that, because there were a number of projects operating to re-set the way BP worked in the aftermath of the Deepwater Horizon accident, this particular focus was called Values & Behaviours and I was the project director. To be honest, I always referred to myself as leading the Values and Behaviour work, not as a project director, as this wasn't a one-off, it was about embedding a refreshed set of expectations and then adjusting the system to ensure they became part of the ongoing agenda and decision making. But sometimes you need to be pragmatic and a chameleon depending on your audience (more on this in Part Three, Chapter 14).

Remember, the first priority task of the culture lead as they start out is not to prove the specifics of the opening diagnosis, such as exactly what the culture is today; it is about achieving clarity on what the CEO, senior team and culture lead agree the remit is. Without clarity and alignment on that, the work will be off on the wrong foot.

Let the diary rule

The contract between the top team and the culture lead on the time they meet is key to being able to make and maintain momentum. This commitment should be settled as the work is being set up.

I cannot stress enough just how important it is to get the time in the diary and the regular rhythm with the most vital decision makers at the start. To ensure the continued support, commitment and focus (or at the very least to know where it is and isn't) then regular meetings need to take place. The culture lead needs to come back to the top team for specific decisions that are going to require 'having their back', as change is uncomfortable. Given that this is a difficult topic to really build and then maintain momentum on, don't leave the meeting setting till decisions are imminent. It will always be too hard to break into the ongoing operational agenda. Plan it out upfront – believe me, there will always be something to be heard, shared, challenged, and decided upon every time one of the meeting times comes around. It keeps the topic front of mind, and it helps everyone keep current.

And in terms of risk management around momentum for the work, without having clear times in the diary, it will be a struggle to be able to move things significantly forward. To make the shift around culture, a few eggs will need to be broken – meaning that some uncomfortable truths may need to be pointed out, some new ways of working instilled, people's behaviour called into question, and so on. The chief coordinator of this work needs to be able to know they have the support of the CEO and their direct reports in following through on their remit and that means ahead of time, that person should outline these sorts of expectations and the kinds of actions they'll be taking in this regard. If they don't have the support, because the top leadership isn't aware or at least informed, then they may be surprised. The top team needs to be at least aware, even if quietly they are uncomfortable too.

Lock-in slots on the agenda for the year ahead, as a regular item; then there is the opportunity. Don't simply hope and leave it until everyone believes there is a particular decision to be made or backing on a specific issue. It's too late then.

It's a key signal that this work matters, or not. If there is a failure to commit to regular sessions between the top team and the culture lead, then this work isn't really that important.

Case Study

With the BP work we agreed up front we'd meet each month. It wasn't that we defined how long to meet for each session, or a year-long plan of what would be decided at each meeting, but that this work would be part of the regular agenda when the top team met, for as long as it took to define the target culture and to make progress on embedding it.

I found that I worked much better towards timing deadlines than to a plan of activity. I also found that it helped the top team think about the work differently as they knew it was here to stay and not just a flash in the pan.

For all organizations I have advised since, I have become something of a dog with a bone around dates. Without the top team dedicating time to work on this and to make decisions to support those coordinating the efforts, then the work drifts. It sounds bureaucratic, but it's essential. Think of the corollary – if the boss doesn't make time to focus on overall performance, then it will drift. It's as simple as that. It otherwise sets the signal it's not that important. What's on the agenda matters.

Declare an approach

Agreement on the remit of the work and role of the culture lead are precursors to getting started. But so is the approach to change (see next chapter: Turning everything on its head). My experience of how to shift culture, and thereby the advice throughout this book, is founded on a philosophy of behavioural economics, that change happens best from within, going to where people are and what motivates them, by shifting all parts of the system, by recognising it takes time and repetition, and that it's never really done.

As a result, if you are the culture lead, the way you carry out your role will differ from that of a more traditional project manager. It won't involve updates on your adherence to deadlines for your planned activity, but focus on what success looks like and how the system is shifting to move towards that. Take the time to discuss what this will look like in practice with the CEO, and any particular sponsor in the senior team you may have. Provide examples of how it will work, how you will work, what they can expect to experience as you lead this, so that, even if they don't feel entirely comfortable, they know what to expect.

For some, this will be a leap of faith. So expect some pushback, and be prepared to have to continue to justify why you are leading the work the way you are. But don't brush over this and just hope others will know by osmosis how you plan to lead the work. That's being an ostrich with your head in the sand. Face it up front and commit to over-communicating, not under-communicating. (For more detail on precisely how to do this, see Chapter 13: Adjusting the focus).

At a glance

Resist the clamour for immediate action.

Agree the modus operandi – give it real time (set dates), get specific.

Don't generalise, agree each element – the remit, the role, the change approach.

9

Turning everything on its head

Changing, or simply managing and maintaining a culture is strategic; it's not a project with a tidy budget, a start and end point or a precise return on investment. If you think of it that way, you are off to a losing start.

People don't behave like spreadsheets or machines.

They exercise choice when they come to work. They don't always follow orders, but instead often find their own workarounds. They think for themselves, and their logic, ambition, definition of success and overall rationale will all be different. Whatever your direct role in this work, overall the goal is to architect a shift in behaviour in order to drive predictability to underpin the business, not build a bridge or any other inanimate object to engineering standards based on proven laws of physics.

So it's a bit messy, can be somewhat unpredictable, and is very definitely not an exact science.

Behavioural economics is the root of the approach here; people do not make average choices. Traditional economic theories often start with the premise that 'faced with full market knowledge, people will make rational choices'. In reality, even faced with exactly the same visible information, individuals make different choices based on perception, bias, ambition, past experience, assumptions, sentimental value, mood and so on. It's a rational and logical choice to each individual, but it's based on much more than commonly available data and it often results in a different decision from someone else.

Behavioural economics – An illustration

Imagine that you have bought a lamp for your living room for €150. A couple of days after placing it in your home, a friend comes over. They adore the lamp and offer to buy it for €400 as it's something they have been searching for but never found. You decline, even though you paid less than half the amount.

The rational economist would weigh up the cost and benefit and declare that the predictable and logical choice is to sell the lamp and make a profit. But you don't. The financial gain on the lamp is outweighed by the sentimental value attached to the lamp. You have only owned it for a few days, but you have become so attached to it that it would feel too much of a loss to give it away. That decision may seem totally illogical and irrational to the other person, but to you, it's perfectly rational and you have weighed up the value clearly.

What the other person cannot take into account or put a value on, is the sentimental value to you. That's the root of behavioural economics – we are all different, we don't make 'on average choices' from the same data, because our 'data' will always have different nuances to it (sentiment, ambition, mood etc). It's never simply the overt numbers that all can see and are freely available.

But that is not to say that all is lost. The behaviour of an organization does not have to be uncontrolled chaos that cannot be guided, nudged, manoeuvred.

Far from it. It absolutely can be. It just takes a different approach; one that requires some thinking – in fact a lot of thinking, very often, stepping back, assessing where you are, working out what's really going on, what's working and what's not, listening, feeding back, adjusting.

It's a craft, not a science, but very definitely not simply an art.

For behaviour to be shifted into new habits, or maintained in a way that is directionally consistent or predictable, it means recognising that this is not about precision, and not about something being produced and completed. It involves going to where people are and creating a pull from them, not a push from you. For behaviour change to be real and sustained, there must be a sense of ownership and incentivized choice for all involved.

It must start with the organization, not with yourself, understanding what makes others tick, what will incentivize and motivate them to do things differently. Telling someone to behave in a certain way isn't going to work.

Traditional project management themes must be turned on their head.

There will be resistance, and it's important to have some clear guiding principles for how change really happens as well as having a frame to help others make sense of where you are and what the change looks like. Others need to have confidence that there is a master map and it makes sense to someone who is overseeing and leading the work, even if not to them.

> This confirmed my long-held suspicion that many people use spreadsheets as an alternative to thinking.
>
> RICHARD H. THALER,
> Misbehaving: The Making of Behavioural Economics

Meeting resistance

If this all sounds a bit philosophical and vague, there are a number of principles to work from that sum up this different approach, outlined below.

Just recognise there will be battles ahead to gain trust and confidence from others that this will work.

Precision and tangibility are so often bedrocks of corporate mindsets and wish-lists, but this approach is working from exactly the opposite. As the CEO or a member of the wider leadership, don't bury your head in the sand and pretend everyone's with you.

For the culture lead specifically, find your narrative about your approach, hold to it, don't waver, be consistent, transparent and confident in your philosophy about changing and managing a culture. But don't hope you can rely on persuasion. Those who understand the approach don't need to be persuaded, they have already bought in, and those who are creating the resistance are only likely to move towards you over time as they see results, or, crucially, as they see others they regard as influential, supporting this. But you can provide them with some examples to help build their trust.

Are there parts of the organization where you've tried something out before and seen the results show up down the line in business results? Do you have examples from other organizations where they have followed this approach and the results are clear? Use these, providing as much data as you can as evidence. Those who are creating the resistance are, more often than not, those who are comfortable with specifics, data, numbers, predictability, starts and ends: meet them where they are at. Give them data.

With your knowledge of the organization's politics, target key influencers who are on board and ask them to advocate the work on your behalf to those who are putting up the most resistance. They are more likely to find success than you are in the early stages.

Case Study

I was asked to be a judge for awards around business psychology; specifically in the category of change management. The finalists seemed to me to have been screened somewhat in a traditional sense. Most of them had focused in their entries on budgets, plans, structure: the change team's overall activity to drive any shift in culture.

I judged the entries from my guiding principles of how change really happens – has the system shifted, how was progress measured, what was the feedback from the organization, how much track record could the entries show, what was the role of the coordinator?

It was clear to me which were the most successful examples – and it wasn't the ones which focused on the activity maps and how fast they'd done the work. But when it came to the awards it emerged that I had scored very differently from the other judges, who had indeed given points for budgets, plans, structure, activity.

Now this may not be filling you with confidence that my approach has merit. Needless to say, however, I have been invited back to be a judge again as the organization valued my thinking (and I have to say, I think agreed with me). I have adopted the same approach for this year, holding to my view about change and how it happens. I know it works, because I've led it this way and continue to do so, and see the results. I had requested that one of the entries from the previous year that I had scored re-submitted this year and suggested some of the areas for them to focus, if it was going to really make a difference. They have re-submitted, they did focus on those areas, and the results are moving much more effectively in the right direction.

Guiding principles

These principles are illustrated in much more detail throughout the chapters within Part Three but as a summary cheat-sheet, the key ones are here to reflect on and get used to before you dive into the detail later in the book.

1. Time not speed

- You can't shift a culture overnight. We all know new habits take a long time to bed in, no matter what they are. And this is about behaviour, which is something we've individually developed over years. If it's never been focused on before in an organization as truly critical, then it takes even longer to move, as on top of behaviour change, there needs to be trust built that it really does matter and that the focus is serious and will be consistent.

- Processes may need to change to reinforce the expectations. Changing performance management or recruitment approaches is a time-consuming task and it's likely to take at least two if not three cycles to get it working as you'd want it.

- Time needs to be made, carved out, for everyone (not least the top team) to spend time on the topic of culture. Not just once, not as a fad, but as part of how the organization delivers its strategy.

- And all of this is on top of the time it really needs to take to define the culture through a set of words that become expectations.

2. System not initiative

- Aligning a culture is not a one-off project but an ongoing investment

- Behaviour can't be declared, the environment needs to adjust to make it unavoidable and inevitable

- Adjust the system: many dials need to be lined up in the same direction to drive the outcomes, not just a single activity (see more detail in Chapter 13: Adjusting the focus)

- Track progress on shifting that system i.e. monitor whether the dials are lining up, rather than simply tracking whether the outcome of an updated culture has been achieved. Focus on leading indicators for a long time: only then can you be sure the lagging indicators are predictable, not simply luck or serendipity. If you think of a house; focus on ensuring the plumbing is working rather than simply testing the temperature of the radiator.

Case Study – Icelandic youth becoming the healthiest in Europe

In the 1990s, Icelandic teens were among the heaviest-drinking youths in Europe. Analysis revealed correlations between lower rates and four key factors: participation in organized activities – especially sport – three or four times a week, total time spent with parents during the week, feeling cared about at school, and not being outdoors in the late evenings.

Instead of simply sharing public communications on the hazards and downsides of youth drinking, the government put together a long-term plan for focusing on creating an environment where teens were receiving natural rather than artificial highs.

1 It changed laws (raising the age for buying tobacco and alcohol, requiring parental organizations to be established in schools, introducing late night curfews for teens).
2 Created a different incentive environment (increased state funding for sports, music, art, dance and other clubs.
3 Underpinned with communications (healthy living, benefits of sport).
4 Enrolled everyone (annually surveyed the teens on their habits and preferences).

Between 1997 and 2012, covering 15 and 16-year-olds, the percentage of teens spending real time with their parents on weekdays and the percentage who participated in organized sport four times a week had both doubled.

Today, Iceland tops the European table for the cleanest-living teens.

- The percentage of 15- and 16-year-olds who had been drunk in the previous month plummeted from 42 per cent in 1998 to 5 per cent in 2016.
- The percentage who have ever used cannabis is down from 17 per cent to 7 per cent.
- Those smoking cigarettes every day fell from 23 per cent to just 3 per cent.

Focus on the system and shifting that – the outcomes will start to emerge.

---

3. Flexi not fixed

- Culture, and thereby behaviour, is an emotive issue. What may seem logical in a plan, may not be borne out in reality.

- Don't set the activity in stone: go where the energy/traction/take-up is (as long as it is progressing towards the goal). Two workshops may be planned in but there is a demand to run ten; participants may want the thiry-minute engagement session to run for an hour. This means the activity will take longer than had been planned; but do the ten and take the hour. When there is demand, harness it.

- Similarly, don't hang on to something because conventional wisdom says it should work; seek feedback from within the organization to understand what isn't working and what might work better. Cut the things that are gaining no traction, particularly if it means more time and energy can be devoted to where the engagement already is.

Case Study – Be flexible, and be willing to adjust established processes, to keep things fresh and momentum strong

---

An American software technology company was tracking employee feedback quarterly, using a process of about 50–60 questions each time. They started to notice survey fatigue. But with 'employee-led' as a foundational focus for the company, they knew that tracking employee feedback remained essential. Through a wider process that involved discussion about alignment across their culture they adjusted their process: two questions, every Friday, different each week, taking ten seconds to answer a week, instead of the twenty-five minutes each quarter. The variety reignited people's interest in the process and the company. The trust index across the company rose as they became more attuned in real time to how employees were feeling and the live issues they were dealing with.

---

4. Hands-on not hands-off

- Sitting on the sidelines shouting instructions won't work. This is all about sleeves being rolled up and getting stuck in. The culture lead specifically should make sure they are visible, on all forms of media.

I don't mean purely in person, but via any communication channel that employees operate with. They need to be seen as the focal point, the one who can answer all their questions, listen to their feedback, assure them there is a plan. But other senior leaders need to pile in and be active too. This can't be left to one person.

- This work is not simply a faceless, organizational initiative, but one that has personal ownership and a 'face'. This makes it more real, tangible, and dare I say it, believable. Visibility of the culture lead is foundational. Again, other senior leaders can't hide and must make a concerted and consistent effort to be visible and vocal on this topic.

- Connect things up, use, influence, adjust and amplify existing processes and activities: don't create new ones.

Case Study

In my work at BP, I made a promise to anyone I was coming into contact with that I would respond to them personally within 24 hours if they contacted me directly, no matter where in the world. Whether that was by an email, a text, internal social media such as yammer, or a phone-call. I was trying to build trust, to ensure I would be hearing real stories from people, and at the same time creating not just trust in me, but belief that the work had momentum and their voice would be heard. It took a lot of discipline to do this and meant I was rarely 'switched off'. But it did pay dividends in the form of ever-increasing participation and stories, as well as feedback and ideas coming forward more proactively. Anonymity when sharing feedback upwards was always part of my offer, which some took up, some didn't bother about. But knowing it was there, seemed important.

---

5. Everyone, not the few

- Coordination is required centrally, but it's orchestration of the organization's activity, not the activity itself. If you are the culture lead you are the air-traffic controller, not the pilot of the planes. You can't do activity that changes people's behaviour; your role is to connect processes, communications, expectations, to create a system that funnels people into a narrower definition of what's desirable and required to be successful individually and as a business.

- Engagement – all employees are part of a focus on culture: involve them – or fail. Orchestration can't happen without the organization taking part. So expect something from colleagues; or see the work remain as a set of words on the wall. You can't tell people how to behave and expect them just to do so. They are adults, they choose to work here (it's not prison, it's not slavery), so you need to work with them, join them up, ignite them, not dictate to them how they should behave. They need to take part, not just observe from the sidelines, and that means engaging them to want to do something, or at the very least know that they have to or fail. This is so much more than broadcast communication, it's marketing not selling, appealing to what motivates people to create a demand for the culture to underpin the organization's activity.

6. Family not friends

Use your own, use your best, don't outsource. It's so tempting to call up the nearest or best consultancy house to ask for the solution, the brains and the arms and legs to come and help us, to 'sort our culture out', 'fix the way we work'. It'll be quicker, it'll be the industry solution, and while it may cost, at least we know it'll be done properly.

- But the cost and investment required here is not $ or the 'right answer', it's time, brain calories, focus and really looking in the mirror with true insight. That's most effectively done from inside. External stimulus can be hugely valuable, to provide advice and a sounding board. It can also help prevent organizational blindness by pointing out things that internally you've stopped noticing. But, the best resource to lead the work, to front it up, is internal.

- While often a shift in culture involves overcoming long-held norms and habits, these can be issues that are not visible to those who are unfamiliar with the organization. They may lie just beneath the surface of what is immediately visible to others. But it is essential to recognise these in order to be able to ensure they diminish. Insiders are required.

Case Study – A number of lessons learned

It was only on the third attempt to lead this work, while I was at BP, that I started to really make progress. The previous two attempts, when I look back, involved me walking into every pitfall that I have outlined in this book. So, it is not without real-life experience that I am sharing these guiding principles.

I have learnt the hard way about setting goals not writing plans, about taking time not going for speed, about being flexible not wedded to activity, about using internal resource and only having a small, focused team while engaging the wider organization.

When I first was given the chance to lead this sort of work, it was 2007. I set off exactly as I would warn against today. I created a team, I sought out an external consultant, paid them to spend weeks understanding what was going on (instead of me and internal people doing it) and appointed someone in a dedicated project planning role and instructed them to develop the timeline for activity to ensure we would get to a defined culture by a certain date. We tweaked the plan constantly, to ensure it all hung together and looked like it would work to precision on the timing, what we needed to get done and how much it would cost. It looked like any other business project plan, and that was entirely the intention. All about inputs from this team, to ensure we delivered the activity we needed to get done, to achieve what we'd been asked to do. I wince when I think about it now.

I had missed the point.

We had all missed the point.

We were approaching this with a push mentality, not a pull. And too much of it was focused around defining the words, not thinking beyond that. It was a bit like preparing for a moonshot.

My engagement with the senior team reflected the plan and the detail inside it, not the goal of what we really needed to deliver, which was a culture aligned to the business need.

I wanted to move fast, to ensure that we were able to get the senior team to agree to a load of activity speedily, in case their attention waned (I clearly didn't really think they'd fully bought in, if I'm honest). When I look back I think I was so focused on persuading them by using as much data as I could, by proving my plans were detailed and precise, and thereby credible.

Whether they were scared off by the cost, or the complex way in which I was describing what had to be done, or whether (more likely) their mindset was 'let's get this fixed', I don't know. But when cost cutting was introduced, I was asked to scale back, terminate my team, cut all external consultants, think about a different approach, and do a 'light touch' re-work, taking a look at what was currently there, and then tweaking some words.

My approach to the issue had been naïve. I had spent too much of my focus trying to ensure the fragile commitment of the senior team would not be sent off track, and had put a plan together that was just another initiative. A complex one. A costly one. With lots of people, and lots of outside help who were remote from the organization. We'd spent three months, and hadn't yet engaged the wider organization, other than by external consultants interviewing people about the current culture.

I look back now and it was crystal clear that the approach wasn't going to get sanctioned. And thank goodness. We had nearly created an industry of activity, all focused on defining words, keeping the senior team comfortable, and not on getting to the root causes of where we were and where we needed to go.

Learning to drive

With the guiding principles above, you have the bare bones of a philosophy with which to effect change around organizational culture. Put that together with the traits required to be the culture lead (pragmatism, patience, passion etc) in this sort of work and you have the makings of an approach that can really make a difference.

But how do you keep track of where you are in the grand scheme of things?

How do you know what stage of progress you are at and how do you explain it?

Are there different stages of change that you need to keep track of and move through so you can know when your culture is really what you need it to be, or is it just one continuum?

There is much more detail on specific things to measure later on (in Part Three Chapter 16: Filling buckets not spreadsheets,) but knowing roughly where you are on that change map, living out that new culture, requires a map itself: something you can use to explain to people very simply and relevantly where you are on the journey.

In its simplest form, managing organizational culture, whether as a focus in itself, or whether it's about a particular form of that culture, is all about learning new habits, new skills. You don't know how hard it is until you try, then you take ages to practise and improve, and after a while it becomes second nature.

Then someone comes along and shows you that they've become better than you, you have relaxed into sloppy habits, the context has changed and you need to relearn or at the very least refresh.

Learning to drive is a great analogy here; and in particular learning to drive a manual-drive car, one with gears.

You have been driven around by someone else for years. It hasn't really occurred to you how it works or what's involved; you just know it's been getting you from A to B. You may not even have paid much attention to being in the car at all.

Then you reach that moment when you first sit in the driver's seat; only then do you realise that you had gone through life with no idea what was involved and you realise you have much to learn and practise. Fast forward a few weeks or months and you are now thinking hard about and practising the different processes: 'mirror, signal, manoeuvre', 'squeeze the pedals don't push them', and so on. You also have to learn how the car works and what the rules of the road are (literally), so that you are equipped when something goes wrong and following a consistent set of principles. Eventually you pass your test and you're allowed to drive on your own. But you still have to think about the new habits in order to make everything work properly; it's not coming naturally yet, and you work hard to improve for a quite a while. It gradually becomes second nature and over time you no longer are conscious how it works or which foot is on which pedal. A few years down the line you have a minor accident, or you receive a speeding fine, or you are sent on an advanced driver's course by your employer – and then you are shown how sloppy you've become as you have relaxed into your own driving habits. You also realise how many of the rules of the road you've forgotten or have even been remembering wrongly. A refresher programme is an ideal way to re-engage with how things should be working and where your gaps are.

It's the same with managing the organizational culture and any change required to ensure you have in place what you need.

Illustration of learning a new skill – learning to drive

1 **Unconscious Incompetence** – you have been driven around for years, but not taken much notice of what is going on. Simply you have moved from A to B with someone else driving.

2 **Conscious incompetence** – the pedals, the gears, the width of the car, the directions, the rules of the road. So much to learn and so much to coordinate all at once; so any mistakes.

3 **Conscious competence** – hill starts can be executed, reverse parking can be mastered, but slowly, carefully and with a lot of effort.

4 **Unconscious competence** – This may happen long after you have passed your test, when you are no longer thinking about the clutch or the signposts, but they have been incorporated into your everyday habits.

Unconscious incompetence

Whether you are an organization that simply hasn't considered culture as a core business driver, or one that has paid no attention to the culture you have or need, or one that considered it's 'just the way it is around here' and hasn't thought to refresh or track the culture for a while, then you are most likely in the 'unconsciously incompetent' phase. It's a phase where the topic of culture and what it might take to ensure it is aligned to underpin what you need to deliver, just isn't on the radar screen.

The big picture – recognising where the organization is

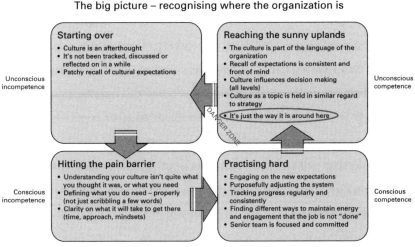

FIGURE 9.1

Conscious incompetence

Recognising there is a problem and that work needs to be done, being clear what the remit is and the scale of the task, and then committing to focusing on it for a good long while, are key to this stage. Facing the uncomfortable reality that your culture isn't what you need, or that you may not have put it as a priority until now, or both, cannot be rushed through in a couple of weeks. Organizations typically don't spend enough time sitting in this position, wanting to push on to simply writing a new set of statements, publicising them and declaring a new culture is in place and that it's going to be taken very seriously into the future. It's during this phase that some stakeholders get a bit jittery and question whether this work really needs to be done, or whether there are other things to prioritise. It's an uncomfortable phase for all; it feels messy (and it should) and as if nothing is really happening. We like to kick on, get into action, make plans; but that is just what this stage is all about. Making plans. But not the sort with spreadsheets and workstreams. It's all about the set-up, recognising the scale of the gap or misalignment and being clear on the challenge ahead.

Conscious competence

This is the practising stage. Whether it is working to put culture more front and centre, or also working hard to align your culture with the one you need, it is all about being conscious and purposeful to make this happen; practising the new way of working. It doesn't matter so much whether people believe and own the change yet, as to whether they are doing it, and that together with senior leadership, you recognise that as an organization you will spend quite a long time in this phase. Don't assume you can rush through and declare victory within a few weeks. You may declare it, but you won't have got there, in spite of signals around quick wins. It's not yet embedded as a change. New habits take time to form – and stick.

Unconscious competence

Oh, the joy of being in an organization where culture and strategy are on an equal footing, where the language used is the culture that is publicised, where stakeholders in and outside the company recognise decisions being made that reflect the purpose, the strategy and the stated culture, where colleagues use the values of the company to help them make the right decision when things are unclear and there are difficult choices to be made. It does happen. And it is the goal that you are trying to achieve.

And once you get there, it will require less overt intervention than the earlier stages; more a case of maintenance to ensure things remain this way.

But watch out for the danger zone that can come after a long while of operating in the Sunny Uplands of an embedded culture. Like strategy, you don't state it once, embed it and then leave it. It needs updating, ensuring it is still relevant and appropriate, and it requires some high-level intervention periodically.

It's a bit of a continuous loop, and that's why on the diagram it shows 'it's just the way it is around here' as the danger zone. When that becomes complacency, where everyone considers they've mastered the culture topic, and no focus at all is required, that creates the potential for bad habits, inconsistency and the need to head back to the beginning again for a re-set. Memories become a little blurred about what was really meant, what was really said, who had really agreed to what.

We all know that anything left too long without checking, runs the risk of going off track. Back to house maintenance again. Do none at all for a long period of time and you run the risk of some problems lurking under the surface, growing larger and creating a bigger problem down the line.

Once you've got to that stage, you have effectively flipped over the line back into unconscious incompetence, and you'll need to pick it up again, take a look at your current culture, your stated culture, your strategy, the system you have created to reinforce expectations and work out where the gap is. It may not take quite the heavy-lifting you had to do in the first place – a light touch review perhaps only required – but my point here is that this is a loop, a cycle, that requires maintenance.

And so it begins again . . .

At a glance – Not your usual project management approach

Think 'behavioural economics', not traditional project management

Prepare for meeting resistance

Hold to guiding principles:

- Time not speed
- System not initiative
- Flexi not fixed
- Hands-on not hands-off
- Everyone not the few
- Family not friends.

Manage organizational culture as you would helping others to learn a new skill; like learning to drive.

Long-formed habits and ingrained skills become sloppy and outdated without maintenance and regular checks.

Adopt the same attitude: don't rest on your laurels, or you're back to the beginning again.

PART THREE

THE HARD YARDS

10

A long, hard look
in the mirror

Too often organizations launch into a focus on culture by heading straight to defining a new one.

That's all very well, and of course being clear what culture is needed and expected as an organization to be successful is a critical part of the work of managing culture. But purely starting from there and then working towards it is a bit like starting in the middle.

It fails to recognise what the culture is today.

Worse, it declares a signal that today's culture is wrong, off-centre or not working, without having done any checks.

And finally, it takes no account of what's working to reinforce the culture today, formally or informally.

Without this additional detail, it's hard to be able to get clear how many mountains will need to be moved to shift towards any desired culture that you may yet need to define.

To be able to solve a problem, it's important to be really clear what the issue is today and why.

In Part Two, I outlined the importance of everyone being on the same page around the overall task. At least start with a common view of the issue. But from that initial scope, then before rushing off to 'fix' the issue, don't start working towards alignment with the desired culture until there is a long, hard look in the mirror at today's situation. It needs a detailed look. Given senior management can sometimes be shielded inadvertently from the culture in all its glorious technicolor, who knows what surprises this might throw up. And it could change the scope of the task, in fact, it's probably quite likely to.

- There may simply be confusion or misalignment.

- There may in fact be elements of the culture that are exactly what is required, but just not getting into the spotlight and being propagated.

- It may be latent and simply needs to be unlocked and unleashed or dialled up rather than redefined.

- Perhaps most of the organization has the culture required and aligned with what is expected, but that there are a few pockets of weakness.

- It may be that you have just the right culture for where you need to head, but the expectations are the out of date.

- Or it could be that everything is a bit of a mess.

Who knows, until you really take a look and understand what you have today? Recalling back to Chapter 5 about alignment, is the informal out of line with the formal, is the formal inappropriate, or is everything out of line?

Restricted viewing

As the culture lead, going straight to the top and asking for the definitive answer from those who make the biggest decisions may be tempting as the shortest route to the 'truth'. However, asking the top team their view on the current culture is necessary but not sufficient.

As a CEO, you may be clear you know how things stand, but in my experience, the higher up the organization we go, the narrower the feedback we receive on what is really going on, and the harder we have to work to gain a 360°-view. On rare occasions it may be that we observe it accurately, thoroughly and honestly. More often, it is only half the story.

Occasionally, it may be the wrong story and as a top team we are deluding ourselves that the culture is something that it absolutely is not. And it is often because the full, true picture is not apparent. In some cases, it is of course because there are blinkers being exercised, or worse, choosing to dismiss the evidence laid down as unimportant noise.

But often it is due to being slightly removed from the unfiltered truth. The more senior individuals become in an organization, the less often people provide them with unfiltered, unsolicited feedback. When they do, it comes from only one or two levels down in the hierarchy; it rarely comes from the broad span of the organization. As seniority increases, so does the need to proactively seek out and work hard to understand the prevailing culture en masse, not simply one part of it.

Of course, spending time with front line operations and a diagonal slice of all employees may be a regular part of senior leadership activity and provide opportunities for listening, observing, enquiring, but these can turn into stage-managed events, or at the very least formal, public occasions where those who have something to share may not feel so comfortable speaking up. People think hard about the messages they want to send and share – but the most valuable feedback and insights around culture are the ones that are front of mind, observed without preparation, illustrated in the moment.

Case Study

One of the best bosses I ever worked for was in the US. He headed up BP America and I was his Chief of Staff, and as a result was privileged to shadow him, act sometimes as a second-brain, quite often be the sounding board. What I observed was how he really stayed in touch with the prevailing conditions of the culture.

He had started his career in Ohio and worked with a colleague at an oil products distribution terminal in the state. They had kept in touch over 25 years, though their careers had diverged considerably. He moved into more senior roles and was based in several different countries. She remained in her role at the terminal.

They kept in touch, keeping track of what each other was up to, and gradually across the years they fell into a habit of her dropping him a message every few months to provide her views on the company, how leaders were showing up, what needed to be fixed, what concerned her. It was pure, unfiltered feedback and views shared in a private, informal setting. Totally invaluable. She only knew him as Ross, an old colleague, never as someone who could be considered as 'too senior for the real truth', which is sometimes the trap we can fall into.

He told me it was always the most valuable feedback and insight he received as she told him how things really were. If he wanted to find out how well a message had been communicated across the company, or what the word on the street was about a particular issue, he would head straight to his old colleague who pulled no punches in telling him how it was.

On a clear day

There will always be proponents of a scientific, highly analytical approach to assessing current culture. I have found that straightforward observation and enquiry using a variety of sources (quantitative or qualitative) and seen together as a set of jigsaw pieces creating a whole picture, works just fine. This should never be about providing a precise, statistical analysis. It can't be because that doesn't mirror how humans behave.

Establishing a clear, objective, drains-up view of the culture today is a core element of the culture lead's role.

Don't overcomplicate it or over-engineer it, remember this is not a scientific experiment, but you do need to cover all the bases to ensure you have a 360°-view.

What you are trying to make sense of is a mixture of the following:

- Clarity: the level of knowledge and understanding of the formal cultural expectations.

- Perception: a sense of what really matters in the organization; when no one's looking, how do people believe things really work, and who/what do they believe is really influencing decision making.

- Reality: examples of the culture influencing decisions and the way the organization does business.

To do this, I recommend covering the following six routes to gather your data:

Expectations

- Today's formal expectations
- Family heirlooms
- Prevailing conditions.

Experiences

- Employee insights
- Leadership perception
- Customer and supplier experience.

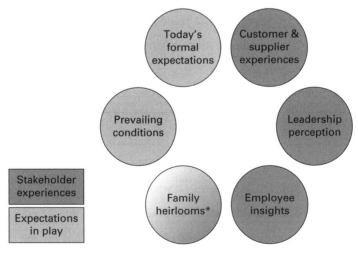

* Some lapsed expectations may still be perceived as 'live'

FIGURE 10.1

Today's formal expectations

This may sound basic, but are you sure you have the full and current suite of material that forms today's formal cultural expectations? It shouldn't take you long, but be sure to be thorough here, to gather what is officially live. It's hard to ask for feedback on the current expectations if you haven't got the full picture to start with. It won't help your credibility in the role either. Having this inventory of current material will also help you later on, should you need to change things and be sure what to retire, and where it sits.

Family heirlooms

As leaders, when we lay out new expectations, we assume the old ones are consigned to history and retired into the past. This may be our own reality, but it is so often not the case for the wider team.

Firstly, the larger the team the longer the time-lag between the leadership communicating something and the front line hearing, accepting and doing something with it. So it could be months before a change is really felt, unless it is managed well.

Secondly, unless we are clear that something is no longer relevant, that it is formally replaced and is no longer valid, there is a high likelihood people will continue working with the old material, particularly if they like it. So the old habits continue unabated – just perhaps a little more underground.

It's therefore important to be clear what sets of expectations are really still in existence across the whole organization. You may find parts of the organization working with material that leadership has moved on from months or years before. This can be more likely the further away from the most senior decision makers you go. Perhaps more recently-set expectations have not yet reached everywhere through the usual inefficiencies of the cascade process, and local leadership are working from the last update they received.

Search the annals to understand what you think is the full picture from the last few years. It may be that there are locally-set expectations as well as centrally-set ones. Make a list and then investigate which of them people are still using. It adds to the picture of what people believe really matters; it will also provide some rationale to why you may have been hearing some of the answers you were in the employee enquiry.

Case Study

I was asked to help a company to define its target culture going ahead. This particular company contained many employees with very long tenures, and hence long corporate memory, so it was important to be alert to some of the practices that may be deeply held.

We created a scribble-pad containing seven sets of expectations – corporate values (three versions back), leadership expectations and extracts from various communications over several years. We went back as far as twenty years.

People were asked to say what they believed was still a live expectation, and what was missing. We also asked them what they believed was still really in operation, even if it had been formally retired. This added to the employee enquiry work around 'what really matters around here'.

We uncovered a diverse set of perceptions about what was considered live, retired or dead, whether those were about local or indeed company-wide expectations.

Prevailing conditions

The processes and systems under which people operate, such as performance management, recruitment, recognition and reward, talent development and succession planning, even the physical workspace, all contain underlying assumptions within them. In a world where the stated and actual culture are aligned, then those processes will have those cultural assumptions woven through them. They will be the very foundation on which they are built. (See Chapter 13: Adjusting the focus, as to how to do this.)

Take a look at a short list of those processes and systems that apply to everyone and ask the person that owns that policy or approach to share the foundational assumptions that are included. For example, is all recruitment requiring a degree, is talent development only for those who want to keep moving up the hierarchy levels, what parts of the organization can take part in the recognition programmes, what are the expectations on line managers in the performance management process, are they tracking only what people do and not how they do it, and is there any follow up?

It may not be immediately obvious to people, including those who are accountable for setting and running the processes, so you may have to work hard to draw them out. But one thing's for sure, whether they are conscious or subconscious, overt or silent, there are working assumptions contained and they are providing signals on the culture of 'what really matters around here'.

Prevailing conditions – example signals sent (consciously or not) and signals received	
Recruitment	Where is talent sourced from and why? What is asked at the interview stage, what is being tested, are people being hired for jobs or careers? While skills may be sought for specific roles, every person has a style, personality, ambition, approach to work. What messages are being sent when people are hired?
Induction	What is taught at the induction process? Those are the first messages people hear on arrival. Is culture mentioned? What expectations are shared? If it isn't, it can be sending a signal that it's not important. What happens in the twelve months post-induction? Is reality lined up with the theory? How is that managed, and who tracks it?
Performance	What is marked up or down in terms of how performance is rated? How seriously and consistently is the performance process followed?
Workspace	Offices or open plan, flexible or fixed, relaxed or formal, noisy or quiet – all of these elements send signals of what matters and how things really work. A workspace isn't simply a 'space' it's an environment that influences how people behave.

Recognition	Who gets recognised? Who is called out formally and who is called out informally? And what are they being called out for? Is there a breadth of areas or a narrow focus?
Development	What training courses are mandatory, and what levels of leaders host them? Who is given training and who is not? Is it a reward or a sanction? Is it internally focused or also externally focused?

Employee insights

The prevailing culture is not purely a fact-based situation. Our own perception of how things work around here impacts on how in turn we make decisions and work. So sentiment matters; hearsay and myth matter. We can all be prone to dismiss people's views of how things really work and what the culture is really like – but again, that is our individual perception. We do need to understand from the widest and most representative audience internally, the sum of all of those perceptions as well as the understanding and awareness levels of formal expectations and examples of what is really happening.

But don't try to gather views from 100 per cent of the organization. Apart from being impossible, it is just not necessary. Remember this is not about total precision but about an overall sense of what's going on, and a representative view can be gathered from around 10 per cent of the employee population as long as it is a truly diverse mix across level, tenure, age, culture, style, skillset – the full gamut.

Do not, under any circumstances, fall into the trap of only asking people you know or only asking people who are positive. All the views make up the whole picture: those you are familiar and unfamiliar with, the positive, the negative and the neutral.

You are trying to gather both an understanding from them of what they believe is the culture that they are working within (the unwritten rules) as well as their awareness, understanding and observed application of the formal expectations through the values, policies and practices.

Remember you aren't simply listening for these three things, but also the level of alignment or mis-alignment between them.

Don't edit what people say; it's not for you to comment or challenge, but simply to gather what you are hearing.

Case Study – The direct approach

I was asked to do a cultural audit of a financial services company. We conducted focus groups with 10 per cent of employees, mixed together in diverse groups of tenure, job roles, gender, nationality.

Each group was asked the same questions about how things are today:

- Name the values.
- What really matters around here?
- How are the values lived?
- How productive is the workforce, on the right stuff?

Rather than ask people in the room, I asked them to write their answers down individually on a post-it note. I wanted to avoid people being potentially swayed by anyone in the room who 'had all the answers' or who jogged people's memories. What I was looking for was their individual, in-the-moment, knowledge that reflected how they act every day; not a referenced, consulted, thought-about set of responses.

Asking the four same questions of everyone meant I was also able to build up both a quantitative and consistent set of results. It's highly repeatable, and can be conducted every year to track progress. A year on I went back with the same questions showing the results in the same format to track progress on some of the issues.

Sometimes, you are working in a context where asking the direct question about today's culture is, for various reasons, difficult. It just may not deliver you very much. Adjust your style of questioning so you can indeed draw out what you need to. It may be just that you need to be a little more subtle.

Case Study – Coming at it tangentially

I found myself in exactly this situation a few years ago with an organization that found it difficult opening up.

Instead of asking direct questions, I gathered together all the different pieces of current cultural expectations as well as the pieces from the past that I had discovered were either held dear or still perceived to be 'live', and put them into one overall workpad. I then asked them for half an hour as individuals to share with me what they liked and didn't like about what was on the workpad and to scribble down their ideas or to talk them through.

Some people took the workpad away and jotted down their thoughts, which turned out to be commentary on whether they saw things working this way today or not. Others sat with me and homed in on particular pieces of the material, sharing stories of how they experienced things today in relation to that expectation.

Through using this approach, I was able to gather a bunch of data on the perception of today's culture, without having asked the question. For many, it felt less like an exam question and something more like a reflection.

Leadership perception

As much as it is important to have a clear sense of what the wider employee population is experiencing as the culture, there are three reasons why establishing the senior leadership view is critical:

- Top teams may regularly spend time on engagement survey results, but don't often spend regular dedicated time on the current culture, so it can be a revelation to all in the team to collectively understand how it reads the current situation (you and others may be surprised to find how different the individual takes are: probably more disparity than had been assumed).

- It provides a clear picture of whether there is alignment or misalignment between the top team's view and the wider employee view. This is in itself an important insight if there is a gap. It provides another piece of data defining the scale of the task ahead.

- It starts to reveal the level of understanding across the top team on how it impacts the wider culture in reality, beyond simply expressing the expectations (for example is 'them' or 'us' used when referring to the culture? A telling sign).

There is no single best method to conduct this enquiry. It depends on how they already work as a team (are there strategic discussions beyond operational meetings, do individuals know each other well, is there trust in the team), and the relationship between you as the culture lead and them (these discussions require trust as you are asking them to discuss behaviour, sentiment, relationships; it can get personal and needs to be treated with discretion and utmost confidentiality).

You will know best how to do this; but take your time. Don't expect to get it done in one meeting. In my experience it can take a few sessions for people to warm up to the topic.

And context matters here; a crisis can speed things along a little, as there is a heightened sense of introspection and willingness to discuss previously taboo topics. If this is something that the CEO has instigated in the normal course of business then it may take a little longer. Some team members will be immediately on board, others will be more sceptical and while paying lip-service initially may take some convincing to fully participate.

Try to draw out two aspects:

- How do you summarise today's culture?

- As a leadership team how well are you living out this culture?

No matter the level of maturity as a team and your relationship with them, it is always valuable to gather individual views separately and to put it together into one picture with responses being anonymous. It creates a real sense of intrigue and engagement to get you started. Never reveal who said what though, even when there is real pressure to share it. The ability to protect people's anonymity around their own views is an important part of the culture lead role. It doesn't make a difference how senior people are; consistency here is key to trust.

Case Studies

1) Normal course of business

I was advising a financial services company. The CEO had decided to assess the current culture following a number of years of recovery post-crisis. The business was now 'back in the game' and on a more stable footing. As the person who had led the organization's performance he had been the focal point for ownership and definition of the prevailing culture. And now he wanted growth, beyond stability.

Given the dominant energy of the CEO and the context of the recent years this was not a top team that operated with much collective ownership of overall performance, or spent time together discussing team dynamics or the organizational culture. It was a collection of individual specialists leading the tasks and challenges in their own areas to deliver the recovery required, under the leadership of an energetic CEO.

As a result, for this group, I interviewed each of them individually, asking the same questions about the culture, the executive as a team, and their appetite for change. Going straight into a team conversation, when this was not at all how they were operating, would not have been productive.

Only after establishing their trust by consolidating all their input into a report back to them and setting that within the context of the wider cultural audit I was conducting across the whole organization were we able to start to move towards a first team conversation.

2) Crisis conditions

When crisis hit a large natural resources company, I was asked to work with them to help them re-set their culture. It was clear from the first meeting that they needed to do this introspection together. I was asked to discuss culture for thirty minutes at their first meeting together (they had only formed as a team formally two weeks earlier, though everyone had worked in the organization for a while so they knew each other).

The session lasted four hours and I didn't do much talking or even ask many questions. Given the context of the crisis and the newness of the team, individuals were much more pre-disposed to look in the mirror personally and to provide candid reflections on their views of the prevailing culture. My role was to listen hard, to guide the conversation a little and ensure there was enough space for all to provide their views without being closed down or drowned out.

On reflection it was part of them starting to form as a team: and proved much more effective than any formally-labelled team building.

Customer and supplier experience

Despite seeking views from a truly representative group of the organization (including leadership) without the views of external stakeholders there is the danger that there are aspects of the culture missing. How does all this perception, insight and expectation manifest itself when the organization operates with its customers and suppliers? What do they experience?

While culture is not the same thing as brand, the culture of an organization shows up to external stakeholders in the way decisions are made and products and services are delivered. So it impacts the brand. Culture is not simply the work environment; it is manifested in the behaviours people exhibit when they are interacting (with colleagues or with external stakeholders) and making decisions. That can be customer services, procurement with suppliers, communications with the press, and so on.

No matter your customer or supplier (individual, large client, SME, government), there will be data you already collect that can reveal what they are experiencing of your culture. Look inside customer feedback for consistent themes on colleague feedback on how problems have been dealt with. You will undoubtedly have customer surveys or supplier feedback. But nothing beats a couple of face-to-face interviews with critical stakeholders who experience the organization from the outside. Ask them directly: why do you deal with us, what are the best bits, what are the most frustrating bits, what do you observe as most vital in the way we work, and so on.

Case Study

At BP, I met with three of its big consumer-facing customers. Fedex took the meeting extremely seriously and I was given an hour with one of the Senior Vice Presidents in Memphis. I asked him to be as honest and open as possible. It was clear the relationship was strong and he really enjoyed doing business with the company. He was complimentary about all the BP personnel he came into contact with and praised them for their passion for their company and their drive to deliver great business. He did, however, say that he felt it would be easier to do even better business if there was a more consistently-held view from everyone he dealt with on exactly how the company worked, who had decision rights on particular issues and that in effect the company worked more as one operation and less as several within a whole. It made quite an impact on the final set of material that was landed. One of BP's values became One Team, and that meeting was an important step in uncovering the need for that to be emphasised as a guiding principle.

Purely understanding your current culture from an internal perspective may in itself have a level of bias in it, and it may be missing much of what could be going on. It can be uncomfortable, but don't shy away from gathering data from external sources about your culture.

Clearing the fog

There are two things in play here, as you pull it all together and work out what you have. The first is to understand what the culture is today as it is experienced by a wide group of stakeholders.

The second is to understand how far away that is from what is stated as expected both formally and in leadership perception.

Making sense

Once you have all your different sources of insight, the task is now to put them all together to create a picture that makes some sort of sense. I regard it as putting the jigsaw pieces together to form the image on the top of the box. Each piece can reveal a lot of detail, or it can leave you somewhat confused; but only when you put them all together and then you stand back, does it start to show you the complete sense of what is going on.

Remember, you are not looking to define every single detail in full technicolor or with scientific precision (if you still harbour this view that you can or that you should, then I guarantee your job will be like painting the Forth Road Bridge where you have to start again as soon as you've finished). You are navigating your way through a complex set of interactions, perceptions and statements to be able to tell a story that is simple, engaging, understandable and relevant.

Test yourself:

- If asked to sum up the culture today in a tweet, what would you say?

- If you meet someone who knows nothing about the culture and you have thirty seconds to tell them about it, how do you explain it?

- If someone asks you to sum up the three culture headline characteristics most prevalent, would you know what they are?

- When challenged to say 'what really matters around here?', how would you respond?

Start simple and expand (a little) from there.

Case Study – Creating the picture on the jigsaw box

When I was doing this work at BP, I had the help of someone who helped us think beyond the traditional approach to analysing data. To this day, I think it's the most effective approach and I use it all the time.

The first step was to go through each of the different lenses and summarise them into an overall usable picture – employee enquiry, leadership introspection, prevailing conditions, family heirlooms.

We found that the best way to do this was to assign one person to each angle and for them to spend a day on their own in a room pulling it all together – a mix of narrative, insights, evidence – however they wanted to best represent the evidence in front of them, but with the context that others, who hadn't seen the material yet, would soon be in a room looking at it to help form overall insights on the culture.

To bring it all together we gathered together about eight people in a room for a few hours and laid out in front of them the material we had gathered from the various inputs.

There was one set of input we did not include: the leadership introspection. Understanding the level of alignment between the wider organization and the leadership's sense of the prevailing culture is a vital insight, so best not to muddy the waters by putting it into the mix at this stage.

Each person in the room was given a bunch of post-it notes and asked to spend fifteen minutes reading all the material in the room and then given a simple instruction of 'write down what strikes you' on your post-it notes and put them up on the wall.

This provided people with free rein to express what they observed rather than being guided in some fixed questions.

Once everyone's input was up on the wall, we then worked together to group them into themes. We weren't looking for answers, we were looking for groupings of things we noticed. This might have been a set of comments on relationships, or hierarchy, or safety, or confidence. Again, there was no format under which items were grouped; we just worked collaboratively until we were comfortable we'd found some common insights.

Now we had our themes: through this approach we had summarised thousands of inputs from employees, observations about processes and systems and legacy expectations into one single group of overarching observations.

The final step of this process was to create a narrative, backed up by examples (quotes, pieces of data), that outlined the current climate.

What we ended up with was not a spreadsheet of data, but a small booklet that was accessible, straightforward, and resonant. A story of the current day culture.

Minding the gap (that alignment word again)

The level of alignment is part and parcel of the overall picture; how close is the culture today (the informal (social and political) parts from Part One) to the expected culture or stated cultural expectations (formal – strategic); and how aligned or misaligned is that with the view that senior leadership holds of the culture today?

- Is everyone in agreement as to what the culture today is; or is one of the starting points to help leaders wake up to issues they either don't see or don't want to see?

- How far away is the culture today from what is laid out as expected? And does that matter? (It does, if you are clear the expectations you have today are the ones you need for the strategy ahead – it may matter less if you know you need a wholesale redefinition of expectations in any case.)

A freshen up or a complete refurbishment?

Culture and strategy should work in partnership if you really want to unlock performance. Think of it like a machine working at its peak potential: the engine is perfectly tuned and the best fuel is in the tank. They don't work in isolation. One impacts the other and together they deliver the overall performance.

There is now a clear view of the culture of the organization today, and an understanding of how far that is what is formally expected, as well as a sense of how well acquainted leadership is with what's going on.

But it's still not clear what you really need to change until you put it into the context of where you need to head as an organization.

To deliver your purpose and strategy, and knowing what you now do about the culture you have today, work out whether you need to focus on:

- Adjustment – the current cultural expectations are fit for the purpose and strategy, but the organization is operating with a different culture, so it's all about working to remove whatever is blocking what you need and reinforcing what is there, not about rewriting words.

- Dial-up – the culture is aligned with the expectations and they are not out of line with what is needed but it all needs to be a bit more emphasised.

- Redefinition – the cultural expectations currently in play aren't going to help you deliver what you need, whether partially or fully, so you'll need to redefine them. Whether your culture needs to shift too, as it's lined up with what you expect today, or whether your culture has elements that you find you will need; you're going to need to work on the definition of the culture you expect in any event.

At the end of this process, between the culture lead and the CEO and top team, there should now be a good sense of what is really going on, versus what is supposed to be going on.

In an ideal world you would hope it is the same. But it won't be.

The reason you are taking a look at this book is because you want to work on your culture and that means you have a gap, some misalignment, somewhere. Either it's in the expectations that are being set, or it's in the way they are being lived out. More often than not, it's a mixture of both.

At a glance – Don't start in the middle

Don't start with only leadership's word on the culture; understand it, but don't stop there.

Dig deeper and wider to understand what's clear, what's perceived, what's happening in reality for all stakeholders.

Take a broader look to get to grips with the formal and informal:

- Formal expectations
- Family heirlooms
- Prevailing conditions
- Employee insights
- Leadership perception
- Customer and supplier experience.

Put the jigsaw pieces together to understand an overview of what you have today.

Assess misalignment: how far today's culture is from the formal expectations and how well leadership is reading the situation.

Put it in the context of your purpose and strategy.

How much, and what sort of an overhaul depends on what the gap is:

- Adjustment
- Dial-up
- Redefinition.

It's most often a mix of all three.

11

Working out what you need from what you have

So, there is now a clear view of what the culture is, how it compares to the formal culture expectations in place, and the extent to which perceptions between leadership and the wider employee base differ on today's culture.

The next step is to agree what culture is needed for the future, and what it takes to get there. There may be some tough choices ahead; and no matter how much input there is from the entire organization, ultimately the final say goes to the most senior leader.

But the process should be facilitated.

This chapter is written from the point of view of some refresh being needed to the desired culture. If you are absolutely clear that the issue to manage is alignment of today's culture with the expectations you already have (because they are still the right ones for your strategy), then you might be tempted to skip to the ensuing chapters, where it's all about tuning into the expectations and adjusting the system to start nudging the organization's behaviour.

If there is a rising certainty that refreshed expectations of some sort are required, this is a chunky section designed to help you through 'so how on earth do we start defining what we need?'

I refer at the start of the book to organizational culture being a craft; not as borderlessly-creative as art, nor as structured and precise as science; but the balance in the middle where judgement and feel are layered on top of analysis and expertise.

Just so, in the definition of your expected culture.

Pulling together everything you have today, amalgamating it into a new written document, summarising with slightly catchier words and rejecting the pieces you just don't like is not going to cut it. A compromised, theoretical approach will deliver a compromised, theoretical result. A set of words that has come about in a few emails, a couple of senior management discussions and hasn't created any real reflection or discomfort, will result in something that no one does much about. Because the process to arrive at it hasn't much mattered.

Whether you are working to amplify what you already have, or whether you need to refresh and update your cultural expectations to better fit with the future direction of your organization, just like strategy, it involves a process, time and effort.

That process has two parts to it:

1   Alchemy (deciding on the scope and mix of ingredients for the content).

2   Voices in your head (strategies to uncover expectations you need).

1. Alchemy

Something so simple as a few words to define how you need people to behave and make decisions; seriously, how many factors need to be considered? Can't we just crack on with discussions and see where we get to?

In my experience, unless you consider upfront some of the different angles of the material you are producing, you run the risk of spending an awful lot of time down the line fighting about just these specifics. When people can't quite agree on the content, they'll end up fighting about the number of words, the grammar, the level of aspiration. As with so much of the culture work, take a step back before you start and work up a draft of the different constituents. Everything may not yet be pinned down, but the culture lead, the CEO, and also any particular sponsor of the work within that top team, have had a discussion about the elements below, so that there are similar expectations at the outset as to what you are working towards producing.

Set the frame at the outset.

a) How much is enough?

The amount and detail of material you need to specify will depend on your context.

Take the example of an organization post-crisis and having reflected deeply on who it is and where it's heading. In effect it is starting again, wiping the slate clean and trying to re-set an organizational culture that is a departure from today – in which case you may need to produce more rather than less. You'll need to refresh or reconfirm the role of the organization, as well as the cultural expectations within that. In that case you'll have to refresh the purpose, mission and cultural expectations. Using the values as the short-hand for those expectations, you may have to define not just what the values mean in the organization's context, but also the behaviours that bring them to life and ensure consistent understanding. If this material is due to replace old material, being more, rather than less specific, is important (as well as ensuring that the old material is vocally and formally retired – see Chapter 12 for details).

This is an extreme example, but whatever your context, before you pile into defining the cultural expectations you are going forward with, take a step back to agree what form that material will take and the extent of it.

Are you just creating values, associated behaviours too, a purpose and mission, or simply redefining and clarifying the current set?

The choices to make here even come down to whether to use single words as your values, or phrases, or even simply have a narrative, something akin to Johnson and Johnson's credo, in place since the 1930s.

There is no right or wrong answer, but be clear what it is upfront – what to include and not include and more importantly, what is up for grabs and what isn't.

Decoding cultural content: What is it we're trying to clarify, redefine, or draft from scratch?*

Purpose
The reason for which something is done, created or exists. Not easily achievable, but will always be true e.g. a hospital's purpose

Diageo
Celebrating life, every day, everywhere
Alibaba
Championing small businesses

Vision
An aspirational description of what an organization would like to achieve or accomplish in the mid-term or long-term future – what's possible in the long run in terms of how it impacts the world it operates in

Amazon
Our vision is to be earth's most customer centric company; to build a place where people can come to find and discover anything they might want to buy online

---

Mission
A *mission* is not simply a description of an organization but an expression, made by its leaders, of their desires and intent for the organization. The purpose of a *mission* statement is to focus and direct the organization itself. It can be a strongly held aim, or calling; a tangible, possibly hugely audacious goal, that proves you're making your vision a reality and you're on course with your purpose e.g. NASA's 1960s mission to land a man on the moon

Visa
To be the best way to pay and be paid for everyone, everywhere
Walmart
Saving people money so they can live better
Google
Google's aim is to *organize the world's information and make it universally accessible and useful*

Values
These are principles that reflect a judgement of what is important. They are vital and lasting beliefs or ideals shared by the members of a culture about what is good or bad and desirable or undesirable. Values have a major influence on a person's behaviour and attitude and serve as a broad guideline in all situations for making choices

Tata Group
Integrity
Excellence
Unity
Responsibility
Pioneering

Behaviours
The way in which one acts or conducts oneself, especially towards others, or in response to a particular situation or stimulus. They represent the values that are laid out as guiding principles. Behaviours translate values into tangible, observable and measurable elements that can be implemented, assessed and improved, working with behaviours can avoid ambiguity

Competencies
A combination of observable and measurable knowledge, skills, abilities and personal attributes that are used to define expected employee performance and ultimately result in organizational success

Organizations rarely externally publicise the specific behaviours or competencies they look for from employees. These are most often held internally and for specific performance and development.

*All company expectations in public circulation October 2018.

I am not suggesting you need to be defining all of these; and in fact what we are focusing on in this book is really around the values and behaviours, as the shorthand for your culture in action that is required to deliver your purpose, vision, mission and strategy. But they are listed here to clarify what each one is for, so that you can be sure you have a consistent frame from which to agree the form and extent of the content you may need to reinforce, adjust or redefine.

It's more important that you are clear and consistent on language than on ensuring you have all of them listed out. It's also helpful to be clear what it is you are gathering together when you do an inventory of what expectations you have in play today. I would be very surprised if you don't find that one of the challenges is people aren't clear what is which, or how they fit together. In fact, perhaps some of them don't, as they have may have been drafted at different times, in different parts of the organization, set against different contexts and ambitions and hence may not fit together very well at all. Worse still, they could be contributing towards some conflicting messages about what really matters.

b) Mine or yours?

So let's assume you're focusing in on the values and possibly their associated behaviours – the ideals of the organization by which people should be forming their behaviour and making their decisions, and the tangible ways in which those should be demonstrated in the way people interact and make choices every day. The culture as people live it out and experience it.

But what sort of values are you planning to ask people to sign up to living out?

Do they need to be the same as moral/personal values or do those remain silent?

Are you looking for something that represents the particular character of how this organization works in addition to those values?

Or a mix?

By moral or personal values I am referring to words such as integrity, respect, fairness, trust; the kinds of fundamental principles that we may hold dear in the way we live out our lives. It would indeed be a rare organization that would deny these elements are also fundamental in how they work and expect colleagues to. But that doesn't mean that each one chooses to call them out as their values.

As you start to look at the definition of culture that will work for you, keep in mind which are moral/personal values and which are those that provide a unique reflection of the specific character you need in your organization; and how you are going to express them.

Some organizations do include some of these in their set of values. While they may not appear to be unique to them, if they are operating in a context where such principles are called into question, such as a particular industry with a difficult reputation, a country with different cultural norms for doing business, a market that is not fully competitive, or their own context is one of recent crisis, then such moral values as trust and integrity may indeed be just that; unique and differentiating.

Others choose to hold them more clearly as foundational, assumed, given, or hard boundaries in terms of their licence to operate. They may therefore not call them out as part of their culture as part of the memorable mantra, but state them within a code of conduct, compliance and ethics rules, in their high level statements about purpose, vision and mission, within their annual report overview and many other forms.

If you choose to specify none of them at all, then be sure you address this:

- as you are seeking input from the organization

- as you are working with the senior team to agree what you are defining

- again when you are sharing the agreed desired culture with the organization later on.

I have found that there is a mix of individual starting assumptions in any organization:

- those who expect the organization they work for to overtly reflect personal/moral values in any statement around culture

- those who regard them as a given and who are assuming what will be defined is something that is specific to the particular medium term mission and strategy.

Ultimately, you are asking people to make a choice about signing up to working in the organization, and the principles by which it expects individuals to operate, make choices and interact. If the values you lay out are ones that people cannot sign up to, then they need to choose whether to stay and operate based on these values or choose to leave. If they don't make that choice and you find them continuing to operate by different values, then you need to discuss with them that you will be making the choice for them – and then do it. (Or else you are sending the signal that the values you have stated aren't that important.)

Sometimes a debate can ensue as to whether an organization should expect people to sign up to values that aren't personal ones. So, I would propose you are clear, if you are not expressing these personal/moral values as a clear part of your desired culture, that you ensure your ethics or compliance team holds these are the basis for operating within the at all, and then the cultural expectations are built on top of these.

There are hard boundaries in place through ethics and compliance teams, and HR policies that ensure sanctions for those who step outside the rules in these areas.

Moral/personal or corporate, the values, and thereby the culture of the organization, should not be optional. But be clear as you are working to define them what is called out and what is foundational.

c) It's a given: no need to shout about it?

There are some things in organizations that are so innate and central to the focus of its delivery, its way of operating, its definition of success, or its licence to operate that it seems unnecessary to call them out as part of the culture.

This is a debate worth having.

For example:

- Are you a consumer-focused business where customer centricity is the underpinning of the way you operate?

- Do you operate in a high hazard environment where safety is paramount and without certain standards you don't have a licence to operate?

- Is technical excellence the very core of what you are there to deliver?

In any of these situations, or any others where a foundational priority exists and is held dear in perpetuity, the question remains: do we call this out as a value or do we leave it as a 'given' top priority at all times?

There is no standard right answer, that's for you to discuss and agree upon. But don't duck it; though it will be hard to, as I guarantee someone will bring it up. As they should.

d) Shoot for the stars or be satisfied with your lot?

Once you have clarity and shared understanding amongst the key decision makers on your current culture, you will have a better sense of where some of its strengths as well as weaknesses are. In some cases, you may have uncovered something deeply held that has never been written down, yet forms part of the fabric, legacy, DNA of the organization. And you may also have discovered some significant gaps not just between your current cultural expectations, but your hunch about what you need for the future.

Do you set about defining a totally aspirational culture, one that re-emphasises the good of today (including those elements that may have been uncelebrated to date) or a mix of both?

As with all of these ingredients for the content, it depends on your context. If you are in the process of setting a new audacious mission and strategy, then your starting assumption may be that you will need to express some new, stretchy-looking values that aren't held in the organization today.

Hold on though: don't fall into the trap that because what you need to deliver as an organization is ambitious, that you need ambitiously worded, new values. It could be that the strengths in your value set today ought to be further emphasised to accelerate a particular part of the strategy, or it could be that the definition of that value needs to be tightened up and made more aspirational. Or it could indeed be that you don't have, in your culture today, the right values that are going to elicit the behaviours required to deliver the goals; in which case maybe some new aspirational values are required.

Case Study – It may not be the words that need to change

I was advising a company on how to move its culture from continuous improvement to disruptive innovation. When we assessed the company's values, first assumptions were that they would need to be changed, to drive a shift in approach. We came to the conclusion this was not necessary. Today, the activity and behaviour worked off those values: tomorrow, they simply needed dialling up further, specified with more verve to lay the foundational expectations for what was required.

Moving from low simmer, to healthy boil, if you like.

Much more important was the shift in leadership behaviour and the system to drive the shift. There was nothing wrong with the headline words of the expectations – those simply needed dialling up.

My point here is that there is no one right answer, no off-the-shelf formula, and it needs some real thought about what the organization is trying to deliver, then looking at what you have today in your culture, and being pragmatic. It's very rarely going to require a total removal of everything you value today and to be replaced with something totally new. More of an adjusted blend.

But recognise in the absence of you discussing it upfront, there will be several different views about what it should be. It may be that you agree that until you've worked through the process you keep an open mind, but even having that conversation, will save you process headaches later on. The last thing you need is to be fighting over the ingredients of the cake at the end when you're about to put it into the oven to bake.

e) Pick a number, any number, between three and five

It is a commonly held perception that the human brain can only remember up to five things at any one time. It's not a bad rule for the definition of your desired culture, since you need the organization to be able to remember it, for it to trip off the tongue, especially in the formative stages of it becoming the 'new norm'.

A study of FTSE 100 companies by Maitland in 2015 found 50 per cent of companies held three to five. There were several outliers, most notably one company communicating twenty-seven values on its website.

You may agree on two, you may go for ten, you may choose to simply write a narrative; the important thing here for the wider organization is to consider how accessible and clear the definition of your desired culture will be.

Remember this is something for everyone, for those people who don't have all the context you have, for people operating in vastly different roles; and they need something they can remember, something that provides some key signals, something relevant that helps them make choices, not a coffee table book that requires thumbing through some sort of index to find the key points.

It's crucial to make some choices. It's so much easier just to lump everything you would like into a long list. But resist this. I have been in many situations where a top team is stuck with six or seven values and they would rather simply go with the full list. I always push them to choose, because in doing so, we see whether they really are testing themselves on what matters.

f) Harmony or tension?

Your desired culture should force people to make some choices in their behaviour and decision making. Be prepared as you are thinking about your updated cultural expectations that there may be tension between some of the elements, not just in the choices people have to make every day as they live them. What you are trying to create is an overall system of expectations that underpin and support the delivery of the organization's purpose and strategy. It is multi-dimensional, not one single flavour or answer. In different circumstances some of the cultural expectations will need to come to the fore more than others, and sometimes they may create an even more difficult choice. How do you marry care with commerciality, innovation with consistency, respect with challenge, discipline with creativity, pushing boundaries with discipline?

It comes down to three things, all of which need to work together:

- how well you define the value (or other way you will express the cultural expectation)

- encouraging people to work through with their judgement

- ensuring everyone is clear on the purpose of the organization and the overall vision.

Cultural expectations, particularly in the form of values, do not give you the answer; they provide the frame in which you make decisions. They are the compass when there is no map, the guide when there are no instructions. They should indeed force you to stop and think as well as to be providing a most effective guide, when there are no detailed instructions in place.

Recognise before you start defining your desired culture that you're not necessarily creating a set of words that fit together to create a single viewpoint, but a well-rounded guide for people to make choices in any situation within the organization. Judgement will always be required, tensions may well exist and balance will need to be found.

g) It's just words

In the end, you may well come up with a set of expectations that has a ring of familiarity, at least in the headlines if they are values. Going down the list of FTSE 100 companies a few years ago and their values, it was extraordinary to see how many had the words integrity, respect and innovation. Those were the top three in terms of frequency of appearance. Only a couple of companies had expectations that no one else had.

Does this undermine the value of declaring a set of values at all? If everyone is declaring a set of words taken from a lexicon of about fifty in total, then doesn't it all become a meaningless tick-box exercise and generate more cynicism than added benefit?

On first look, it's hard to argue against that, but there are a couple of things to consider here:

- Tailor your language to your context and who are you trying to recruit and hold onto, as the tone of the words can make a difference to their impression of your organization. If your organization's core language is English, then there are a plethora of words that can be used to provide nuances to other similar words. Take teamwork – could it also be solidarity, unity, alliance or even in French, esprit de corps? (But remember to always try them out in different languages to understand how their meaning may differ slightly. Another reason to think about the specificity of definition, for precision and consistency.)

• This is not about trying to be distinctive from other organizations in the words per se (that is more a philosophical approach around your brand), but about ensuring the content resonates with your organization and that you follow through to ensure they are lived out and become the new behavioural habits. There is nothing wrong with having the most commonly used words as your own values, as long as they consistently form part of your ongoing business focus. In the end, unless you do something with them, they are simply words. Don't confuse the two – one is words on a page, one is what is happening in reality. Working to ensure they are the same is what makes the difference.

2. Voices in your head

So there is plenty to think about in terms of the ingredients for the final material you come up with. Forming something meaningful from all these ingredients, how you make something from this 'Alchemy', must also involve dedicated time with and from the senior management team.

Don't leave it to chance, or the default of meaningless wordsmithing will emerge, based off a bunch of assumptions around aspiration, moral or corporate, number and so on. Set your principles upfront, so that you at least have some sort of boundary to work within. It will also help the team monitor themselves and take assurance from working within some sort of structure.

Have your eyes open to the eyebrow-raising that may happen as you kick off the process with the senior team to uncovering and pinning down your desired culture. Having spent a while finding out what you have and thinking about the sorts of ingredients that will make up the words that you create, some will undoubtedly feel that simply now getting on and writing it is the most effective way forward.

Of course, at some point this will need to happen, and it may happen very suddenly and very simply (more later – in fact through this process it should feel quite obvious when you get to content that works).

Omnipresent context

But I would never propose simply writing the material without taking a step back and starting from the purpose and strategy of the company: the culture that is required is the one that underpins that delivery. They define the broadest context in which it must operate.

Is it clear what the purpose and strategy is? Are you sure everyone in the team is clear? The mantra of 'never assume' pops up here again. Draw out the key tenets of purpose and strategy so that it's clear in the room the context in which these expectations need to sit. Surfacing the level of alignment on ambition and the scope of the challenge, is important before any pens are put to any pieces of paper.

Ask the audience, phone a friend or go it alone?

You will also need to consider the extent of involvement that the wider organization has in defining the final material. Is this a purely top team exercise (I advise not) or one where views from the organization are going to be invited – and to what extent?

You could choose to:

- just push ahead, you have enough data
- selectively invite contributions
- seek active involvement
- crowd-source the answer.

At this stage, you have already asked colleagues about today's culture, so they have given you clues as to what is working and what gets in the way. That is valuable to understand today's challenges but it may not be set in the context of the strategic direction and purpose of the organization, and so doesn't give you much in terms of what the culture needs to be to ensure business delivery. For some, they may have set their input in the wider context of the whole organization, but more often as individuals we think about such issues within our local working environment.

But you have already engaged them in some sort of discussion about the culture, retreating now back into a darkened room with simply the senior team to define everything would be a backwards step on engagement and trust, as well as simply missing out on some fantastic insights and ideas.

Scales and funnels

There is no fixed time for how long this should take, or indeed, for the different parts of the process within it.

As I have said before, this is a craft, not an art, not a science. So any process you run to reach a definition for your desired culture will not be precise and never exactly the same as any other organization. At the same time, it will require some sort of process to ensure you don't end up in ever-decreasing circles of frustrating wordsmithing that results in a meaningless mush of compromise and generalisations.

The precise process you use is best illustrated by case study examples, as I have provided here, but if you are looking for a rough checklist, then I have found the following frame useful.

Cheat's checklist for arriving at a set of expectations

Before you even start	Is the strategy clear? If it's not, go back and get that landed first. Culture without direction is Brownian motion. Don't reinforce, adjust or define any culture without having a clear strategy in place first.
Wish lists	Ask the organization its wish list culture to deliver the purpose and strategy. Ask top leaders individually the same question.
Consolidate into key themes	Consolidate these together with areas of strength and key insights from the current culture that are essential to deliver the purpose and strategy. This creates your map of common themes (strong current DNA, common wish lists, contradictory themes).
Rating on a scale	Define a scale for each theme (e.g. what could it mean) and ask top leadership individually to point to where it is today and where it needs to be. Amalgamate individual leadership responses into one scale for each theme and share back in a working session with the top team – to find an agreed 'desired destination' for each theme.
Test with the organization	With your map of themes and associated desired destinations for each one, head back out to test informally with colleagues (use your culture network here, amongst others) – making it clear that this is about input from the organization, not a decision point.
Make choices	Top team working sessions until choices are made to reach your agreed number of common themes. From there, agree the words that define the value for each theme – being clear to make choices to ensure you arrive at no more than the maximum number you agreed to have. It's all about choices.

Stress test with reality	Check against examples of real life situations that have happened already in your organization to stress test whether these expectations are practical, whether they can be committed to, whether they will help people make more of the choices you need, to deliver the strategy.
Settle for nothing less than 100 per cent	Don't settle for 90 per cent agreement and support – you'll know when the words are right. If you don't think you know, you aren't there yet.

A caveat here: in defining the culture you need, it could be the case that you end up with only minor tweaks or nuances on today's expectations.

Remember: the culture you need and a wholesale new set of words are not necessarily the same thing. But this process can work in all cases, whether you're stress-testing your current expectations or are clear you need a fresh set.

The three case studies here provide illustrations of the different extent to which organizations choose to involve the people in shaping any updated definition of culture: from none at all, to the fullest extent. There is no single right answer – it depends on that organization's context and current culture.

a. Case Study – Just push ahead, you have enough data

I was working with a bank who had established that their cultural expectations were sound, but the spark that was missing to help fire up people to drive for more growth was the purpose, role and strategy of the organization.

It may sound fairly unbelievable that an established institution could end up in this situation. However, the bank formed part of a much bigger international group that had did have a clear purpose and strategy, but within it, this bank was really trying to find its way after a prolonged period of being, in its own words 'on the naughty step' within the wider group.

In essence they needed to define what winning meant to them and through that give their employees something simple to go for. It was hard to bring the values more overtly to life without clarity of what it was all for.

While in many cases, spending deeper time with the senior team to define 'winning' would have been what I proposed, it was clear to me that there wasn't much definition to do, with only a few pieces of the jigsaw missing. Asking the organization for active involvement on what winning looked like could have been counter-productive. It's one thing to engage colleagues in the culture that is required – that's about how things work and can work more effectively. It's quite another to ask an organization what they think the purpose and strategy of that organization should be. It wasn't going to be a sure-fire way of instilling the organization with confidence in the leadership.

Instead, we looked at the ingredients, the Alchemy, and then worked fast to create something for the team to work from. We knew the values weren't changing (they were the group-wide ones, and needed to be dialled up in terms of being lived). We knew the material was for employees as an inspiration and aspiration, so it had to be short. We knew that rules around conduct were boundaries that also didn't need refreshing. And we were clear what this was not: it wasn't an employee value proposition, or a set of personal objectives, or a pass-fail test. It needed something on growth, something on the role of the bank inside the wider organization and something financial. And remember: short, simple, memorable.

Working with a subset of the team who were in the right frame of mind, giving ourselves a short timeframe, and knowing we had a deadline of an event in the next month where the speaker would be setting the session in the context of what winning meant to this bank; all drove the session to deliver the material in about half an hour. Yes, half an hour.

Everyone around the table agreed it was a working set of words that conveyed what was important and that what really mattered was how it would be woven into communications, decision making and incentives.

Sometimes going back out to the wider organization either isn't needed or won't help. Setting the boundaries, being clear on the ingredients, setting a deadline, in this case, meant quick work could get things moving.

---

b. Case Study – Crowd-source the answer

IBM 2003

The 2003 IBM values jam continues to be referred to in many books covering the definition of values for a large organization. Sam Palmisano was heading up the company and had decided the culture needed a refresh as the seismic transformation of the internet, personal computing and the world of big data created disruption at a never-before-seen pace for tech companies.

He wanted to do things differently. He certainly did.

Using the global location of its employees, IBM held a 72 hour company-wide conversation online, using its latest technology to connect people live, no matter what level in the company, through a giant digital conversation.

The preparation work upfront had been enormous, working out what different threads of conversations to form as the backdrop, ensuring all senior leaders would take part, no matter where they were in the world, and planning to precision that the technology itself would work so that nothing would get in the way of the conversation taking place.

The exercise was less about people being asked words they liked, and more about conversations focusing on the best of IBM and how they needed to work to deliver into the future given the context of the global marketplace.

Once the 72 hours had ended, the team took the material offline to analyse and examine the core themes that had emerged. What topics had created the most traffic flow, what confluence of direction was forming, where was the mix about today and tomorrow.

In the end, the essence was brought together into three final values:

- – Dedication to every client's success.
- – Innovation that matters, for our company and for the world.
- – Trust and personal responsibility in all relationships.

c. Case Study – A (long and detailed) worked example from the inside

An international energy services company was undergoing a five-year transformation; redefining its purpose, strategy, business model, organizational structure, policies and systems, and as a result, taking a deep look at the culture it required to be successful.

The senior management team was clear what its current culture was, both through its own informal observations and through an enquiry I had supported their culture lead to conduct.

Everyone was agreed that it wasn't firing on all cylinders and that the culture was the final piece in the jigsaw of the transformation. What they hadn't agreed on was what that culture needed to be.

The natural default was to take a look at all the different sets of existing cultural across the various pieces of the business (five different sets of values, several sets of local behavioural expectations, all resulting from various different brands being used in the marketplace around the world) and amalgamate them into something singular, taking the most attractive pieces from each.

This was not going to move them forward. It would have been written by consensus, a purely theoretical exercise in summarising and combining and was about getting to something quickly rather than reflecting deeply on what it really needed to be.

Instead, I asked them to do some homework before a working session.

The wider organization had already provided viewpoints on the current culture, the best and most challenged elements of it, the most critical and stand-out aspects of it, and we used these to put together scales of extremes on particular topics.

We called them tensions.

They may have seemed liked subtle differences between viewpoints, but they would make a big difference to decision making depending on where on the scale was agreed to be the desired position.

Each member of the senior team was asked to send back their own personal view, on each tension, covering;

- Where do you think the organization is today?
- Where do you think the organization needs to be to deliver its purpose and strategy?

All the responses were anonymous. This exercise provided two advantages:

- an overall sense of how ambitious the senior team was about the future requirements for the culture
- transparency, as it revealed where the differences were.

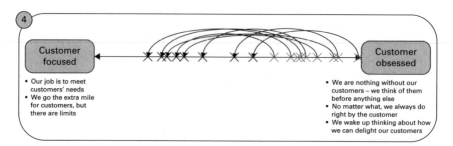

FIGURE 11.1

This is a worked example from that team, showing their individual responses about an element of the existing culture (black) and the desired focus (grey).

On this topic, everyone was directionally aligned. It wasn't the case on all the subjects; in some cases some of the lines were moving in different directions and crossing over, showing that not only were members of the top team not viewing the current situation in the same way, they had different views of direction from here, on top of the levels of ambition.

Each topic was shown back in the room as above, providing the team with irrefutable evidence that there was some work to be done for them to get aligned; and therefore it wasn't hugely surprising that the wider organization wasn't all pulling in the same direction with the same level of risk appetite or ambition.

The agreement up front had been that no more than five values would be finalised, so the team had committed to making some choices. They had been given ten of these 'tensions' to work up in the first place, so it was not going to be as simple as them agreeing just where to align on a particular topic, but to make choices about the most important topics to stress for their desired culture.

At this point we went back out to the organization to test which of the tensions resonated most strongly, asking people to define what meaning they were attaching to them. We also ran this with the senior team.

Once that feedback was amalgamated we were able to group together the ten into seven, as there are always overlaps, and to start honing into what each of these themes would more specifically mean.

Having agreed at the start that there would be no more than five values agreed, while uncomfortable for some as hard choices needed to be made, such a boundary was helpful to really focus the team on what it was they were trying to achieve. Taking them back constantly to the first thoughts they had articulated on what they believed such a company needed to have as its cultural traits to deliver on its refreshed purpose, was essential to keep them on track.

The process was similar to that of a funnel – starting with a wide opening and narrowing down as we moved along, constantly keeping track of where we'd been. It wasn't precise, it wasn't scientific, but by testing, checking for feedback, ensuring honest discussion and forcing some choices to be made, we got there.

And it really did seem obvious once there – it may sound superficial, but the words did just seem 'right' by the time we reached agreement. The iterative process meant that the whole group had experienced a sense of focusing in on something that would be workable. We also knew that the organization would 'recognise' the expectations, since they had been taking part the whole way along. They were well aware they weren't making the final decisions – we had been clear all along – but they could see their contributions and influence reflected in the final outcomes and that ensured credibility.

A quiet moment

Before the final content is agreed, the CEOs must take the material away and do their own research. Build in time for this.

It may seem counter-intuitive for the CEOs to take all that collaborative work away and then single-handedly make their own scribbles; but it's an essential part of the ownership and sponsorship of the material. Of course the whole senior team needs to jointly lead for it, and you can't finalise the material effectively with them only feeling lukewarm about it. However, without the top bosses truly immersing themselves in it and feeling that it's their own, it's like pushing water uphill.

It may be simply that the CEO tests it out with a few close confidantes and colleagues; a personal audit of the process that you, as the culture lead, have been running: their own verification. They may want to spend some time 1:1 with you asking their own questions, providing their own challenge, and really testing the boundaries of what you've coordinated. It may be that they just want to refine a few things and iterate it a bit with you.

Of course, while the CEO is the person running the organization, there may be a bit more formal process to do with any board directors, governors, trustees or others to ensure engagement, alignment or in some cases, that they are in agreement with the content of the material. While the person seen as making all the final decisions may be the CEO, they may have someone they report to who also needs to sign it off. You would hope that there have been conversations during the process to keep them up to speed and to be gathering their additional input, but there may not have been. In any case, this may take a little extra time as they work it around any additional governance required. It is worthwhile asking the CEO as the material is handed over for their 'quiet moment' how their process is going with any board process, just in case this step has been forgotten. The last thing the process needs is to have a last minute spat between the CEO and the board around the words. In most cases I've worked with, it is the CEO who is the final decision maker and their role is to align with and inform the board: but don't assume. It is bound to differ depending on jurisdiction or ownership structure of the organization.

Leave it up to the CEO to choose how they do this. But always set aside time for them to take the material way to reflect upon.

When you get to what you think is the final content it is so tempting to rush to sign-off, because it feels a really important moment, and you certainly don't want anyone lobbying to open it all up again.

There's no need to rush, it's material that you hope will endure. Give the most senior person some time. Let them put their stamp on it – after all, they are running the organization.

Legacy not ego

Before you blindly accept any revisions the most senior leader makes, check back with them as to why they are making them. Act as a mirror back to assure yourself this is about a set of expectations that supports the strategy of the organization, not simply either today's short term challenges or the personal style of the CEO. It is hard to split the culture completely apart from the impact of the most senior leader, but you are looking for material that endures beyond one CEO. It isn't simply 'their culture' or 'their values'. Johnson and Johnson have had their credo since 1930s, no matter who their top leadership is. Now that is a rare event, but my point is that it's worth just doing this check before you finalise, to avoid a culture being redefined in the guise of the top leader's personal style every time they change.

You don't have to like it

Leading the process to uncover the expected culture means you will inevitably form your own view of the 'right' answer. But remember it's not your answer. It is far more critical that the top team agrees on the content, owns it and is committed to bringing it to life, than that it's the answer you believe to be right.

Your role is to ensure that all the different insight and evidence is brought forward, that the challenge is made to ensure all angles are being investigated and that if the top team has stated their ambition for the cultural definition then you push them to follow through on it. But it is not to share your view on the content specifically, other than to share (if asked) whether you think it is aligned sufficiently to underpin the purpose and delivery of the strategy.

It is not easy to keep your preferences about favourite words and the style and tone to yourself, but try you must!

But it does need to be realistic

Remember this is all about underpinning the delivery of your goals and strategy. Culture is not something that sits remotely from your day to day priorities. Whatever you finally agree on as a set of expectations, it will have been a bit pointless if it is not practical. That is not to say it will be plain-sailing from here (see Chapters 17 and 18), but it does need to be stress-tested before it goes into operation.

Before you reach the formal and final sign-off on the words, ask the senior team to test out a few scenarios around decisions. Provide a selection of diverse situations and ask them to use the updated expectations to help them make choices for each one.

Ask whether for specific situations, using the expectations is idealistic, theoretical or insincere. It's best to know right up-front, before anything is committed to, if the senior team struggle to use them. On the other hand, be open to the expectations actually helping to make choices simpler and clearer.

Pick examples that have already taken place, that they are all familiar with, and explore how the decisions would have been made the same or differently, but consciously using the values as part of the decision factors. Try some tricky ones, for example an individual performance management case where someone delivers more than their remit, but does so in a way that seems at odds with the updated cultural expectations. Would the same reward have been provided, would any break on the way the person behaved to deliver their remit be exerted, would they have been supported to make the particular business decision they did? This is not just a good test of whether the expectations are ones that they will all get behind, but whether they are truly up for embedding them into becoming part of how business is conducted.

You may find it's simply a point of definition or nuance, in which case perhaps a small revisit of the words. But if the conversation is already showing that people are stepping back from using them and starting to question whether this is really all about an indication or guideline or direction, then there is more work to do before you sign-off.

The words themselves, and how much appetite there is for them to be embedded, cannot be viewed totally separately. If an expectation is too extreme, then when it is paired back (say, 'relentless pursuit of delivery' to 'focused commitment to see it through') it may solve the appetite to embed into processes and make it hard-edged. So, the words weren't right, but the commitment for them to matter, still is.

Remember, don't accept 90 per cent support on the words. Don't read 'they're OK for now', or 'as long as we remember they're only a guide, not set in stone' as a green signal for final agreement. Keep pushing back until you reach a set that there is real commitment to.

Case Study – Nearly but not quite

At BP, we were tantalisingly close to finalising the newly defined values and their associated behaviours. I was in expectant mood and went into the usual monthly session with the senior team, excited that I'd come out with a signed-off set of words.

Not so.

Everyone was nodding politely as I ran through the content and reiterated the process we'd gone through, all the opportunities they had had to contribute and challenge, how the CEO had spent a few weeks reviewing, and so on.

I asked for sign-off. Silence in the room; until one person said 'you know, I hate to say this as we've spent so long already, but I'm really only about 90 per cent'. At this point, a wave of comments emerged, with people challenging certain words on whether they were strong enough or in fact too strong.

I have to admit I was nearly in despair. Part of me was thinking this was avoidance tactics and that we would never get to a final definition.

However, that sense of being close, but needing a final time-bound effort to land this, prevailed amongst the team. They too had spent so long on this and were now thoroughly committed to making a difference for the whole organization with a clear, simple, fresh set of expectations for all to work from, that we agreed three more weeks, a subset of the senior team and me, to work the content to fruition, covering all the practical challenges and examples that had been raised in the discussion.

We came back three weeks later, no longer polite nodding, but energetic agreement and a collective sense of satisfaction that we hadn't gone with the 90 per cent solution.

At a glance

Uncovering your refreshed cultural expectations is a craft.

If you need to adjust them, be clear on your approach before you start, to:

- Alchemy – structure, mix, length, tone, ambition, number, specificity of words for the content

- voices in your head – an approach for both who inputs and how you hone in towards the desired definition.

Strategy, strategy, strategy – don't start trying to define anything new unless and until you are clear on the strategy they are underpinning.

Alchemy

- How much is enough – just the values, or the whole list?
- Mine or yours – moral values called out or held as foundational?
- It's a given – where to place fundamental priorities.
- Shoot for the stars or satisfied with your lot – ambition not ambitious words.
- Pick any number between three and five – no shopping lists, choose what matters.
- Harmony or tension – tensions are fine, it's a whole system not one angle.
- It's just words – relevant, embedded words are much better than fancy ones.

Voices in your head

- Omnipresent context – purpose and strategy always as the backdrop.
- Ask the audience, phone a friend or go it alone – do you need more input?
- Scales and funnels – start broad and hone in, making choices along the way.
- Don't take shortcuts just because there is pressure to 'agree words'.
- A quiet moment – ensure the CEO has time to mull it over.
- Legacy not ego – watch out for top leader personal style revisions.
- You don't have to like it – the right material for the organization, not for you.
- But it does need to be realistic – before finalising, test for real-life examples.

You may have a Eureka moment – you will know when you arrive at the right mix, it will just feel right. But don't settle for 90 per cent ho-hum agreement.

There is no fixed time period for how long it should take: a tuning-in date may help.

12

Tuning in

It may be a surprise that this chapter is not longer. Isn't communicating your cultural expectations (whether as a reiteration and reinforcement, or as a refresh and launch) one of the most intricate and critical parts of this work?

Well, yes and no.

Yes, in the sense that the tone you set in the way you communicate it is a symbolic opportunity to show the organization you mean it. And yes, in the sense that it will make a big splash as you'll no doubt try to ensure all employees hear the same message at the same time; so it's a real coming together of the clan.

But no, if you think that it's all about the launch. It's only a moment in time. If you don't follow it up with the principles of system change and the way you need to carry out your role as the air-traffic controller of it all, (detailed in the following sections), then it will have been simply a great moment of engagement to energise the organization around an aspirational identity, that either fades from the memory or worse, becomes a focal point for scepticism and derision about 'yet another initiative'. Old, or simply current habits will win through and nothing much will have changed, other than probably entrenching a bit more resistance to change in the future.

As with so many parts of shifting a culture, tuning into it is necessary, but it is by no means sufficient. It is, however, important. I call it tuning in because it is not simply a one-way broadcast of expectations at a single moment. For alignment to really take place, everyone will have to get used to what they mean and how they work with them. It will take some effort, some tweaks, plenty of repetition. Everyone, senior management, frontline, middle tier, will be tuning in. This is, after all, about our behavioural habits shifting to align with a clear set of expectations.

There is no formula for communicating your cultural expectations; but I work off a few basic principles and then design it from there:

- Reflect what you expect

- Everyone at the same time

- Message like a human

- Maximum impact, minimum distraction

- Three equal measures

- All in the same boat

- Trying them on for size

- Withering on the vine.

Tuning in, done well, can make a significant impact and provide a valuable platform. But it needs to be followed through, seen as a launchpad for the culture taking hold, absolutely not 'job done'. All that hard work of uncovering and clarifying what you need is eroded quite quickly if the focus doesn't continue.

Reflect what you expect

Whether you are adjusting things to work more on alignment, reinforcing the current culture or laying out the aspiration, take a long look at how you do your communication and ensure it's all lined up. It's that alignment word again.

Think not just about how you communicate, but who is doing the communicating, and the culture you are espousing through that communication. The way you tune in to the expected culture in itself should be reflective of it.

To take a theoretical example; it's no use sharing a new culture that outlines the importance of agility, collaboration, inclusion, doing things differently, if you wheel it all out in a traditional email and wait for managers down the line to cascade it in their own time, because that's how you have always done it and it's the 'most effective way to get messages out to everyone'. Effective for whom?

What you are signalling is rigidity (not agility), hierarchy (not collaboration), leadership declares and tells (not inclusion) and same old, same old (not doing things differently). From day one you have put yourself at a disadvantage if it's simply seen as another message from management handed out in the usual manner.

Everyone at the same time

An organizational culture is the sum of all interactions, sentiment, habits, perceptions and behaviours: of everyone. And it will take everyone, therefore, to shift it over time, whether consciously or unconsciously. No matter what media you use to engage the organization about the culture that is required, start from the principle that everyone therefore needs to hear it at the same time. Everyone has an equal stake in this.

If you stagger your communication or use a cascade approach you are inadvertently sending the signal that some people don't need to hear it so urgently and that others higher up need to get to grips with it first and then translate it for them.

A perfect score here is near impossible: people are away from work, in a location where connectivity is hard, may have to be spending time with a client at the exact moment of mass communication, or there may be timezone challenges in a global organization. But my principle is that the opportunity for everyone to hear the same messages at the same time should be the focus, and not a drip feed starting from the 'top'.

Message like a human

This is not an investor presentation. It is not a sales-pitch to potential customers. You are trying to enrol existing colleagues over time to change behaviour and create new habits, not to understand return on capital or debt-to-equity ratios. Think hard about the words as well as the tone used.

Your aim is to ensure everyone hears the same thing, understands the same sense of urgency and priority around culture to drive better outcomes. This is marketing not selling; you need everyone to buy in, to be motivated to get after this. So share the message in a way that appeals to everyone.

Make it simple, real and memorable.

Don't be lulled into some sense of it needing to be complex to prove it's right. And don't be fooled into thinking simple means it's in some way too basic. Remember you have been working with all the context and the background for months, but for others this may be the first time they've heard anything about the work. You have about fifteen minutes to capture their attention.

I always find that a good test is explaining to an eight-year-old. If they understand what you're trying to say, then you've got it about right. They hear what they hear, with no context and decide whether it makes sense. And they will tell you if they don't. Use that as a yardstick. It works.

And paint the picture from an employee standpoint; what's going to change for me from today to tomorrow, what do I need to do, why do I need to do it, what do I need to stop doing, when is all this starting, how will I know whether it's taking hold, who is keeping track and when will they keep sharing back progress with me?

Stand in an employee's shoes and work out what you would need to hear for this to make sense, be credible and seem important, if not essential. Provide examples for people in their different environments; how will and does their daily work and decision making need to be for this culture to be alive? And why should they bother?

Keep asking these questions as you plan for tuning in. If you can't answer them, recognise you will struggle to make progress, and adjust accordingly before you start any mass messaging.

Maximum impact, minimum distraction

Finding the best moment to do such a communication is never easy. You are trying to pick a time when people are most likely to be receptive, and that means when there are the fewest other distractions. This is important from an employee perspective to ensure messages are not confused or misread given other context and priorities, and also from a leadership perspective to ensure they have their fullest attention focused on what and how to communicate this.

- Don't try to do this just before annual or quarterly results; the most senior leaders will be totally taken up with numbers and investor sentiment.

- Don't try to do this when the annual employee survey is taking place. People could decide there are too many things about engagement and only take part in one, or focus their entire survey response on the mark left by the big communication on the culture. Worse, the strongest sceptics could take the view that the whole tuning-in exercise was a ploy to raise engagement scores, and 'game' their replies accordingly.

- Be mindful of annual holidays in different geographies and cultures to avoid sharing messages when parts of the population are not in work.

Such a list can leave a daunting prospect. Is there ever a RIGHT time to do this communication?

Well there is never a perfect one, given the calendar of events that any organization has, but my point here is to be mindful of potential distraction pitfalls and to work as hard as you can to time your messaging to avoid them. If you are faced with placing the timing in the middle of some other key events, be very transparent in your communications about this, recognising it is not ideal.

Three equal measures

While laying out the cultural expectations is indeed the primary reason you are planning such a communication, purely sharing this is woefully inadequate. So many people will be coming to this topic for the first time, many will be sceptical, plenty will assume this is simply another initiative from the top, and some will be intrigued and excited. They will all be arriving at it with different levels of context, familiarity and mood. It's therefore important to give everyone the full story, to ensure everyone is at the same level. It doesn't matter whether you think you are repeating it for some: you will be. But reinforcement as well as new messaging is vital for this work to become the new norm. And for so many, it will be a totally new topic.

Split your structure into three equal measures.

Starting point

- Take everyone back to what this work is all about; why it was started in the first place and the rationale for it being important into the future. You know all the context, but others don't. Never assume they do: they won't. Or if they do, they may have their own take on why it's being done. Setting a consistent tone on context is the foundation stone for tuning in. Some call this the 'burning platform for change'. Then share the process by which you have understood today's culture, who was involved, your method and the extent of research you did, and what you found about today's culture. Vitally, be transparent; do not just share the nice gloss. Don't hide the good parts (there will be plenty in any culture that is vibrant, healthy and aligned) but provide an honest look in the mirror. Recognition of what everyone experiences every day is important if the organization is to enrol in any change.

What next?

- Lay out what the expected culture is from today. It's actually often the shortest piece of the communication, even though the starting assumption is it's the main body of it. It's the jam in the sandwich actually – without the two pieces of bread either side, it's just jam. It's one of the tools to help you get to where you need to go, not the destination in itself. Your destination is better outcomes as an organization.

Who/How/When?

- Oh, how we'd all love to gloss over this part and declare victory, as we have now communicated where we need to be. This third piece feels like mechanics; and actually that is what it is: how this is going to work. Don't skimp here. Be clear whether what is being laid out is a reinforcement of today's culture, whether it is a change from what is already formally laid out, and why any change in content might be required, in order to fulfil and underpin strategy. If it is a change, then also be precise about what current expectations are retired or replaced and from when. Outline who this applies to (everyone), when it applies (is it from today?). Your approach to change is vital here; you plan to move lots of dials in the system (see next chapter), everyone must play a part or things won't shift, leadership will be spending X time on this at X intervals as part of their priority set and regular agenda, how people can get involved, who's coordinating it, how long will it take for things to be different, how will that be measured, what does success look like, how will the culture be policed, is it hard edged or optional, how hard is this shift going to be, and how do we make sure we don't move onto something else too quickly before this is done? Is it ever done, or this is dialling up culture to be more overtly regarded as a core part of the way we do business?

- All these tactical details may feel like wading through treacle to you; but not to the employee base who is listening out for whether this really is going to matter and not simply be another top down initiative.

So many questions, but again, put yourself in the shoes of employees who need some evidence that this is going to matter, in order for them to take it seriously.

All in the same boat

Above all, be in this communication together; the leadership is just as responsible as everyone else in creating new habits and new norms; and casts a longer shadow. This is a moment for the pedantry trait: language used from the most senior leadership in tuning in should be about 'us' (not 'you' or the organization or culture in the abstract). Remember it is the totality of all behaviour from everyone – and that includes the very top – so all the messaging should talk about this being for 'us' and 'about us'.

Case Studies – How companies announce their expected culture

Uber new cultural norms

After the growing cultural crisis at Uber across 2016/7 the new CEO, Dara Khosrowshahi in November 2017 made a very public statement about the culture he expected Uber to have. It was a very personal one, shared with employees on that day and then posted in the Uber newsroom and onto the front page of its website. In what was essentially a public letter, he included why he had led the review, the process by which the updated set of values had been defined (employee views had been actively sought), what was vitally important in the company for success and what had had its day, and in summary, the refreshed set of values.

BP

BP was refreshing and reinforcing its cultural expectations in the wake of the Deepwater Horizon accident. More than 3000 employees had, over the previous year, provided some sort of input into the updated set of values and associated expected behaviours. Simplicity, a single, consistent message across all parts of the organization whether doing seismic surveys or selling fuel, and a leadership that was highly visible and human were vital elements of the 'tuning in'. On 29th November 2011 there was an all-employee webcast, not held at the HQ but at a site where more than 5000 employees were located. In the audience were about 600 people from that site who'd squeezed into the lobby where it was held. The top team sat on stage, sharing the expectations, their personal reflections and the importance of clarity and consistency. More than fifty other locations were formally hooked into the webcast with similar large gatherings, as well as individuals being able to log in from their devices, and of course, for those operational teams who couldn't stop their shift, such as refinery or offshore workers, it was recorded and available in full.

Asian investment bank (international subsidiary)

The CEO had asked for a review of the current culture. The organization had been in a recovery period for five years and now needed to turn to growth. The audit I conducted showed that the current cultural expectations needed to be dialled-up, displayed with more intensity, not changed, to achieve this. Nothing was hugely out of line, just on low simmer rather than a healthy boil, which included looking to the CEO for all the decisions. These expectations were the corporate ones, not a local bespoke set. 'Tuning in' in this case needed to signal something different from the usual CEO-centric communication and to begin to reinforce the values expected simply in the way the messages were being shared. I was the one to share the findings of the culture audit, my recommendations and the plan agreed by the CEO and his leadership team. It was an all-colleague town hall and simultaneous webcast, where I was specific on my findings, including shortcomings of the current culture and what needed to be unleashed. The CEO and his entire leadership team were present. Everyone heard the same message, on an equal footing, at the same time (one of the values being Team Spirit).

Case Study – Formal sheep dip

I spent some time with the leadership of a large testing and inspection company, that focuses hard on culture as an asset. It has grown dramatically in the last ten years, partly through an active acquisition approach. It therefore needs to manage the onboarding of large numbers of new employees from acquired organizations. It makes cultural integration a formal part of the process.

Amongst the practices that are held dear are to create a formal ceremony of 'induction' into the culture. It becomes a celebration, and is a treasured part of the sense of belonging in the company. It's public, it happens after a certain period of time, it's not optional, and happens under a consistent process. It's an embedded part of the business process in this company.

Trying them on for size

Tuning in is not complete purely once you have shared the messages to everyone. And I don't mean simply that it takes seven to ten repetitions for anyone to really 'hear' the message. It's more than that. You are asking people to start to get to grips with a clear definition of how things really need to work around here and so far, all you've been able to provide is the context, the words, probably a few stories and a leadership team leaving people with a sense that this is going to matter.

You have been working within this context for months and been heavily involved in the development, definition and implications of this material. You are therefore comfortable with it, eager to apply it and may well struggle to understand why others don't grasp it immediately.

It's not surprising that you may be frustrated, and that others may be a little bemused or reflective.

To be able to do something with this new material, it's only fair people have an opportunity to try the expectations on for size, like some new clothes. How do they work with everything else in your wardrobe? What can you now throw out as you've replaced it, what existing items can this new clothing fit well with? How does it look when you put it all together? This might be a new look – and it might take a bit of getting used to as to how to wear it.

It's the same with a clear set of cultural expectations. Whether they are old ones reinforced, or an updated or fresh set; they need trying on for size.

Colleagues may want to understand where they fit into their own particular team context, really test the messages about what expectations are retired or superseded, have a chance to spend time understanding what they actually mean and don't mean, air their concerns or scepticism about how they will or will not work in reality. That cannot all be done in one set of messaging to everyone. That can only be a start.

They can do this in their own team environment, but it's not fair or practical to assume that team leaders can miraculously get to grips instantly with how this all should work, so it's best to provide opportunities for everyone and anyone to do this in a neutral environment.

Operate a schedule of short sessions where anyone can sign up and turn up. They act as a safe space for people to find out more, hear the context again, understand the expectations a bit more, ask questions about how they should work in practice. Don't make them compulsory; purely voluntary. Train up others to run the sessions as well. Make them informal, lively, honest, short, punchy, and a place where anyone can say anything (as long as it's not with a purpose purely to complain and disrupt for others). Make sure they aren't held only where it's convenient for you to be running them, but where colleagues already are situated. It needs to be as easy as possible for them to turn up.

Case Study

At BP we ran values workshops for the first six to twelve months after the formal announcements. That may seem an unnecessarily long time, but with 80000 people in 80 countries, messages take a lot longer to reach out to the front line than you ever imagine.

The workshops were one-hour long, positioned to be in a lunch break or breakfast session depending on the local working environment. A small number of us (to ensure consistency) ran the first round of these around the world. The second phase involved the values ambassadors network partnering, and then running them on their own (see Chapter 14 for more on culture networks of volunteers).

Each had a very simple agenda:

- 10 minutes – share context and reiterate the specific expectations.
- 30 minutes – human bar chart: with each value heading on the wall, ask people to move to each value according to questions you ask, such as:
  - Which is the value that your part of the business is operating most effectively today?
  - Which is the one that will present the most challenges?
  - Which one are you most confused about?
  - Which one will you personally find the hardest to enact?
- Ask people standing at each value to provide reasons why they are stood there and to give examples.
- 15 minutes – further questions, ideas as a result of the exercise.
- 5 minutes – wrap the session.

Having no presentations (we merely provided everyone with a 15 × 10 cm laminated version of the expectations), keeping the sessions pacey, and the very act of participants standing and physically moving to a different position meant people were really listening and thinking. Being able to observe other viewpoints and hear their stories also reinforced that there was no right or wrong answer.

Withering on the vine

Tuning in takes significant coordination across the organization to do really well. It can be extremely resource intensive. A few weeks beyond this spotlight, the post-adrenalin anti-climax kicks in, new priorities emerge that have immediate deadlines, and stories of quick wins and positive feedback combine to create just about the most risky time in all work around culture; the post-launch dip, from which it can be hard to recover.

The key is to prepare for it and work hard to avoid it. As you are designing for the tuning in, look ahead and create the next six months of rhythm, not just the day and immediate aftermath. In Chapter 8, I referred to the diary with the senior team being such an important thing to get agreed in the early stages. It's at these sorts of moments that this truly matters. Don't plan the time in with the senior team only up to and just after the tuning in; plan it in beyond that, otherwise I can guarantee there is a serious risk of you never getting time on the schedule again, no matter how enthusiastic everyone is. If you have a volunteer culture network (and I recommend you form one – see Chapter 14), this will not be so difficult to achieve as their role starts to become increasingly impactful around deepening the tuning in, as they root out great stories to share, support their leaders to translate and apply in their local environments and learn from each other.

For peers who will be partnering with you to adjust processes they too will have a lot more to do once the tuning in is done, so the danger isn't as much with that group either.

It lies with your visibility with and commitment from the senior team, and thereby the impact that can have in the wider organization. Make it unavoidable for their attention to be swayed onto other things, as it'll be impossible to gain it back.

Case Study – Global conversation . . . but it has to go further

---

I worked with a leadership team a couple of years ago that really did make the time, dive into the process and engage employees on exploring and defining a clear culture that they believed would enhance delivery of their purpose and strategy. We were all clear on the remit, on the risks and on what it would take. The tuning in was creatively led from within, with a video hook-up across different sites with senior leaders located in each place, with employees from right in the heart of the workforce sharing and celebrating the new beginning of what was to become their new shared culture. The office space material was abundant and consistent in its visibility. There was real momentum.

Then a difficult business issue arose as the external context shifted. This took over the short term focus for the top team, and when the person I was advising to lead the work chose to leave the business those two actions together meant there was no catalyst for the senior team to find further time for the culture work on their regular meeting agenda. They forgot they weren't done. They passed out the role of the change lead to different people, way too early, before any processes were truly embedded.

It's an example of an organization that released its values to a big fanfare, adjusted its performance management, then let the foot off the gas. I have been tracking and observing from afar, in the meantime. The breakthrough in the performance they were expecting has not happened yet. It's a huge opportunity missed.

At a glance

Reflect what you expect.

Everyone at the same time.

Message like a human.

Maximum impact, minimum distraction.

Three equal measures (it's not just the content of what you expect that matters).

- Starting point
- What next?
- Who/How/When?

All in the same boat.

Trying them on for size.

Create a rhythm for the senior team, to avoid withering on the vine.

13

Adjusting the focus

After all the work to have understood your current culture, agreed what the required one is, and engaged the organization around aligning the two, isn't it just a case of putting in place initiatives, expectations, incentives and sanctions and then tracking whether the behaviour now exhibited by the organization represents the culture required?

That would be the wrong thing to focus on at this point.

Of course, in the long run, the true measure of success is indeed that the actual culture reflects the expected culture and that it is underpinning and reinforcing delivery of the strategy.

But for the first couple of years, the focus needs to be on shifting the system; all the cogs and dials inside that create an inevitable environment of that culture coming to life. The environment has to shift to underpin and drive this outcome, for it to be sustained longer than the push of the 'we've got new values' period.

It's a bit like dieting. If I want to be five kilograms lighter, I eat less, measure my weight and after ten weeks declare victory. I am five kilograms lighter. Within three months I am back to my original weight. While the focus is on, I achieve my goal. But this has been an initiative, something outside of my regular habits, something to specifically achieve a goal. I have not changed any lifelong habits, not adjusted my mindset to make this a new way of life, and when I take the pressure off myself, I go back to my original habits. What looked like success is short-lived and I am back to square one. If I am to sustain being lighter, I need to make eating less, or eating differently just the way I am; and that means adjusting the food on my regular shopping list, size of my meals, maybe even the times I eat. And sticking with it. Perhaps it will even take a measure of not buying any clothes above my target weight, so providing an incentive to keep my new habits.

It's the same with culture. It's never one thing that will drive a sustained shift in habits, behaviours, perceptions; but a prolonged effort at creating new habits, through ensuring that the environment is different, subtly and overtly. As long as that environment is lined up to underpin the culture expected, eventually that culture will emerge as inevitable.

So focus on shifting the system to make new habits inevitable. And as I say, it's never one thing, it's a mixture of all of them. An adjusted lifestyle to ensure a lighter me, for good.

You'll see examples of the expected culture in place and be seduced into thinking it's all taken hold. It most likely hasn't. They are positive signs, and as part of shifting the system, make sure you highlight and celebrate them, but don't rest there.

Similarly, if you don't see examples of the expected culture in a short time frame, then if you are only focusing on that, you could be fooled into thinking it's too much of an ask, it's the wrong expected culture, nothing we are doing is working. But actually it's most likely to be that there aren't enough signals across the system both incentivising and restricting people to start behaving in that way. We all know persuasion isn't sufficient. We have to work harder at structures as well as beliefs. Colleagues may still be getting to grips with what this all means and trying it on for size.

In short; working to ensure the environment reflects the cultural expectations, and that these expectations influence the core business and the way decisions are made, eventually will drive consistent behaviour to follow. But missing this step out, and purely focusing from the start on whether people are now behaving as per the updated expected culture, means you run the risk of this being the equivalent of a fad or yo-yo diet. Once the next initiative comes along, people will revert back to their previous habits once the focus is off.

Shifting the system

What does it take to shift the system and ensure the entire environment reinforces the expected culture? Is it simply changing processes, or just ensuring leadership act as role models?

It's those, and more, and the combination of them all. Like an engine. It all has to work and fit together to ensure the best performance. It may work, but if a number of things aren't quite right, it will underperform slightly and in fact, there may be the odd warning light that comes on.

I have found six different elements that really are the essence of what it takes to have the best chance of the culture you expect being the culture you enable. They need to work in concert with each other, feeding in and out of each other, joining up to create a consistent, aligned system of expectation and reinforcement.

1   One clear message

2   Leadership effort

3   Policies and processes

4   Symbols, signals and practices

5   Everyone in

6   Guiding compass in decision making.

How thick is the red thread?

The aim here is not to force a system where everyone is a clone, but to create a common red thread that runs through the fabric of the organization around how to behave, work and make decisions around here.

The six elements to shift the system to the culture you need don't change, no matter what your context – they are good for all seasons.

But before you step into driving the implementation of this red thread, determine your plan for just how much is completely common and consistent, and where local context and tone should or can exist.

In effect, how thick should this red thread be?

Do you need to encourage an emphasis on different flavours of the culture in different areas of your organization? Or do you need consistent application of the culture across the teams and with quite some specificity?

It goes without saying that various parts of the overall organization will be further away or closer to the desired culture than others. That determines the scale of the task and focus of the effort required.

But it does not address how thick the red thread should be: how far into the daily decisions as well as identity the expected culture needs to pervade.

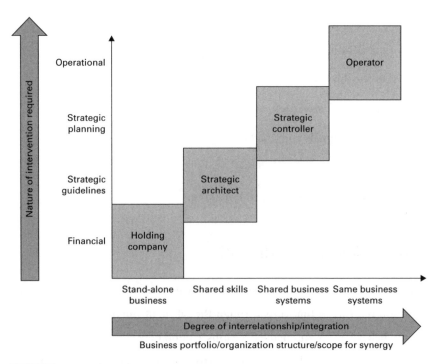

FIGURE 13.1

Source: Goold, Campbell and Alexander – Corporate Level Strategy

It is the operating model that signals the depth of application you need to run to.

At one extreme of the spectrum (holding company), the sector and brand of one part may bear no relation to other parts of the organization, with stakeholders not even knowing they are part of the same overall entity. In that case, your common red thread may be microscopic, perhaps only at the highest level of something like business integrity and ethics. Defining and embedding a common set of values here may not be necessary or even appropriate. In fact you may want very different cultures with little commonality.

Come in a little bit from that extreme, where people do know they work for one overall entity, but work in different, related organizations within the overall corporation and it may be that it is enough simply to operate to a very light touch of common culture with high level definition and then applied locally with more differentiation.

Case Study

Burmah Castrol was bought by BP in 2000. It has formed a very successful part of BP's business since then. While there is some movement of talent between the Castrol team and the wider BP, there is a sense of belonging and brand identity that is slightly distinct from the 'bigger corporate'. The working population involved a core bent towards sales and marketing, and b2c markets, more so than BP which is more b2b and b2g in the majority. In tuning in Castrol to the BP plc values and supporting the teams to embed them as part of how they work, it was important to pay attention to how they should be interpreted and applied within that environment. And it had been vital to engage and enrol those teams in the definition and reality checking of the values themselves.

In agreeing the common processes across the whole of BP into which the values would be woven, Castrol was a bottom-line test. Would it work there? And for the content of the values, while that would not be altered for anyone, the way they are applied could be nuanced. In Castrol, people live out the product brand values externally, but the way they make their internal corporate decisions is absolutely the BP way. It's all about the balance, according to the balance of the operating model.

On the other hand, if your operating model is much more like an operator, where to all stakeholders (internal and external) this is a unified team with one way of doing things and one sense of overall identity, standards and decision making, then the depth, breadth and consistency of application of the expected culture will need to be much greater. The red thread may be more like a red rope. Not only should the application of the content of the values be more common, the number of processes that are common and consistent is likely to be more, and the cultural expectations have a bigger playing field to operate within in as one set.

In reality, the vast majority of organizations operate somewhere in between the two ends of this scale, with both commonality and different flavours (as per the Castrol example). So you will need to have a strategy for the depth and specificity to which the six elements below run.

The key principle here is to line up the breadth of your red thread with the way your whole organization is run.

That word 'alignment' again.

So now to those six elements.

1. One clear message

It may seem obvious, but having one message, only one, that doesn't change (not even a bit and I really do mean not even a bit), on repeat for a long time, that is the shorthand for the culture you need and expect, is the foundation of this effort to shift the overall environment.

We would all prefer to interpret it, put our own spin on it, change it a little to better suit our particular environment and personal objectives, pick the bits we think resonate the most. Be honest, we've all done this at some time or other when a new message or expectation emerges. But here, precision and consistency is essential.

The shorthand for a culture should be the values that define it. Be clear, crisp, unswerving in your consistent communication of them, including their definition. This is a time to be pedantic (see Chapter 7). Pedantic about the detail and how it won't change. At all. Don't overcomplicate the message; you don't need to. Simple, clear, direct. Repeat, ad nauseam. At that point, you may just start to have traction with other people starting to believe it may matter and that it may be not be a flash in the pan.

Case Study

At BP, with operations and employees in eighty countries, finding one set of words that could be shorthand for the culture was a challenge. Holding to those words not being changed, in an environment where individual flair had been very much celebrated, was another one on top of that.

To overcome this we:

- Tested the words across the twenty-two languages we needed to publish them in to ensure meaning was not altered, and on the flipside, that it was something that could be tangibly acted upon a particular culture. It meant that one of the words was changed at the last minute given its translation into Spanish had negative connotations.
- Created a strict protocol on the design format for the values (including font, colour and order) for any communication of them from the corporate centre.
- Agreed with company-wide process owners who would be taking the new values into their processes as part of the overall shift, that the design protocol would apply to the communication around those processes as well – to create the sense of a system being updated holistically.

My role was to be the steward and guardian of the words; to be the pedant who would not allow even a comma or a tense to be changed in any of the values definitions or the behaviours associated with them.

The Communications team was a key partner in this work and without them we would not have been able to follow this through.

---

2. Leadership effort

Leadership role modelling can be an off-putting term. It creates an expectation that the senior leaders are perfect examples of the living culture already and therefore reinforces that acting just like them is what really matters. Everyone know that isn't accurate, as like everyone else, they are flawed individuals.

Calling it 'role modelling' can lead to one of two extremes:

- Either leaders avoid trying altogether because they know they are not very skilled here and are nervous to look foolish. As a result they leave the impression that this doesn't matter at all or it only matters 'for others', as carrying on with their own way of interacting is absolutely fine.

- Or they provide examples of where they are bringing the culture to life but it is so glossy or watered down that it appears like wrapping paper and has the same impact – scepticism that this matters at all.

What is really needed is leadership **effort**, and that means:

- Individually being honest about where personal gaps exist, working to act differently to remove these, and seeking feedback along the way.

- Individually and collectively making this part of the overall business rhythm and agenda by weaving it into existing meetings, structures and ways of working with their team and within the top team.

Case Study – Preparing properly

I was supporting a leadership team of an energy services company as they prepared to release their updated cultural expectations, through a refreshed set of values, to the wider organization (the 'tuning in' step). Instead of the CEO being the sole communicator, the whole team was up for sharing the new material. The CEO would host and set context, followed by an individual team member talking through one value, what it really meant and where they personally had strengths or gaps in using it as part of their everyday decision making and interactions.

Some of them found the preparation simple, and in fact were unscripted on the day about their own strengths and gaps. Others asked for help in working out what to say, and felt more confident with it written down.

Their approach made a big impact:

- Showing up as a team rather than purely the CEO showed their joint ownership and commitment.
- Being willing to be honest about where they found some of it difficult built more engagement and trust than them purely espousing 'how everyone needed to be'.

Case Study – A little every day makes a lot of difference

As a board member of a number of companies, I spend time on visits to various parts of the businesses to be able to pick up a real sense of the operations. On a recent visit for one of the companies, the local leader was working hard to deepen the culture of valuing marginal gains in a very difficult market environment. The work was all about delivering service, based off strong processes. Visual management boards were part of every team's operations. Everyone in the office could see what was going on in each department, hour by hour, day by day. But how could she reinforce this need for marginal gains? She took a simple approach: she wanted fewer emails across the office environment. So she deliberately asked for no more updates, and simply made sure every day she walked the floor to update herself by looking at the visual management boards for each team. Email traffic reduced into her, people observed that if the leader was working this way, then it must be serious. It further reinforced the sense of the importance of the visual management boards as a way to illustrate where small gaps in process still existed and marginal gains could be achieved. A walk around the office every day – as simple as that. But done consistently, without fanfare, just as part of how she worked and thereby led.

Case Study – Fallibility is human

At an American software technology company, employees were surveyed about their managers in terms of employee experience. Each people manager confidentially receives a level for their own performance. Through culture workshops they were encouraged to share them with their team as well as their managers. On an ongoing basis, use of a real-time feedback tool is encouraged, which managers can also see. Transparency provides a further emphasis that culture truly matters as part of performance.

3. Policies and processes

What channels many of us down certain decisions and patterns of behaviour are the structures within which we work; the policies we need to abide by, and the processes we follow to get things done.

These include all aspects of the employee lifecycle (recruitment, performance management, development) and others that equally apply to all people in the way we work every day (a code of conduct, recognition programmes). Each of these contains certain assumptions. They may not have been established with a deliberate set of assumptions called out, but they all contain them nevertheless.

When hiring someone, if faced with two equally qualified candidates, how is the decision taken to recruit one or the other? If cultural fit is an overt measurement point then it's all clear (your task is to ensure that's the same cultural fit as you are trying to effect across the whole organization). But if there is no clear direction on how to make the choice, what are the factors that are influencing the final decision? It could be someone's individual biases about style, or rationale about the cultural fit that is required in practice. But you can't be sure it's consistent, or in line with the culture you need to build. To be sure, you'll need to make it an explicit part of the hiring requirements that the candidate will be able to deliver within the culture you have laid out. So the cultural expectations form part of the definition of capability requirements for the role. They form part of the process by which recruitment decisions are made, formally; not as an optional add on.

Case Study – Incorporating your expected culture in processes that touch everyone

An American software technology company I have spent some time with ensures that not only does every applicant have a skills fit interview, but also a culture fit interview before they can join the company. This is not about seeking clones, but checking alignment around the values for prospective employees. Questions such as, 'how far would you go to sell a product to the customer?' (testing alignment with the value of integrity) and 'what do you do to have fun?' (fun being another value). 'One person's fun might be fishing, someone's might be going to festivals every weekend. We don't care, but we want them to know that fun is important here.'

This is the same for other common processes that affect everyone.

Remember you are the air-traffic controller in this process of managing and shifting culture. Your role is not to be the one who adjusts these processes. Your role is to contract with those individuals who have the accountability for writing and running these policies and processes to agree how and when they are going to adjust them to ensure they explicitly reflect and reinforce the cultural expectations laid out via the shorthand of the values.

Case Study

At BP we redesigned performance appraisal to specifically incorporate the cultural expectations as part of performance. I partnered with the company's Head of Reward to ensure this had the maximum impact. The updated process was communicated together with the 'tuning in' of the values; all as part of one set of messages indicating the whole system in which we work was shifting. The message it sent was that this was joined up, consistent and serious. Not just a set of values on the wall, but that they were now going to be part of the way our performance was tracked. All of us, all working off the same form, with consistent expectations.

The Head of Reward took ownership of designing the new approach, while I held the ownership of 'the words' within. Together we worked up ideas of how this might work, but we had to be very clear who was accountable for what. I was not updating the process, but was the guardian of ensuring that the process would reflect both the importance of culture as an element of performance and the cultural expectations would be effectively incorporated into the process.

Adjusting how performance is appraised and on what criteria, can be one of the most impactful processes to adjust. As individuals, apart from our sense of recognition for a job well done, it hits the money in our pockets and our ability to progress and develop. For a company with an engineering and number-driven set of skills, this had to have some hard edges.

The outcome was one common structure for performance management, one common form for everyone, no matter what their role. Simply in itself this was a huge signal around one of the values that the company was seeking to reinforce – One Team.

We didn't get it totally right first time (see more on this in Chapter 17), but the clarity we had about who was doing what, and the overall purpose meant that we had a joint ownership of solving the challenges. It took three cycles before we were happy with it, three cycles before the process was really working and we could see that the behaviours associated with the values were:

1. Consistently applied in objective setting.
2. Effectively being taken into account when rating performance, individually and versus others.

---

4. Symbols, signals and practices

These include a vast array of the every-day, and are the essence of how the regular rhythm of work gets done. They may appear more subtly than policies and processes, including how meetings happen, who takes decisions and how they are communicated, feedback processes, how networks of people get together and with what level of influence, the communications approach and content, recognition events. It is a mixture of the overt and the subliminal, but really does represent the fabric of our daily interactions and activity.

Some people will see conscious signals of the expected culture, others won't even realise the signals it sends, or certainly won't be reflecting on them specifically. But that should not deter you.

Your role is to ensure they are lined up.

These practices, by their very nature of being the fabric rather than the loud noise of the way work gets done, are hugely influential. They are the habits formed over many years; it's just the way things are around here.

Case Study – Understanding what people believe really matters around here

---

I was conducting a culture audit for an Asian investment bank. As part of the process to understand how people perceive the culture as well as how things were really working, I asked individuals within a focus group to write down the top three cultural expectations in the organization. I gave them no further clarification than that. I wanted to understand what they really thought mattered; what cultural signals were they experiencing.

The pattern that emerged was reflective of their recent experience – transformation and delivery to recover from a crisis, a real focus on compliance and a new energy around diversity. None of this was surprising, nor was it at odds with the values that were on display across the company. Everyone could relate to the values, but the most recent focus, reinforced by the way decisions were made, what work was prioritised, the most prominent messages they were receiving from the leadership, were overshadowing the values, acting almost as a dampener to keep them on a low simmer rather than a healthy boil. The next question I had asked was what the values were. Recall was very good, but the other signals around recovery, compliance and diversity were more amplified. In their experience every day at work over the recent past it was the issues they had seen emphasised.

There was nothing wrong with the organization observing these elements as really mattering. Leadership was delighted that people were taking them seriously. But it was a wake-up call that the expected culture (as defined by the values) was too much in the background, while the initiatives came to the fore as just that – individual initiatives. What was really needed was for people to observe the initiatives in the context of the expected culture and that they were a real representations of it coming to life.

More joining up had to be done. More context and an overall narrative was required.

Communications is one of the more overt elements of this system of symbols, signals and practices. Be careful not to confuse its influence with its ability to be the 'fix' for shifting a culture: communications by itself cannot shift people's behaviour through persuasion alone. But it can certainly play a significant role in shifting people's perceptions of what leadership believes really matters. All channels matter and again, consistency across them is vital.

Case Study – Managing the message into the fabric

I formed an agreement with the Editor in Chief within the Communications team in BP to have the expectations around culture both reiterated as an important driver of performance and the values themselves called out within the communications.

Consequently, employees saw a consistent set of messages coming through CEO staff emails on quarterly results or strategic announcements across the company, and through to communications on annual processes such as certification to the code of conduct, employee recognition awards or the annual performance appraisal cycles.

For senior appointments and job moves, a reference was made to the particular values that individual displayed as strengths and attributes for the role they had performed and were about to carry out.

Always the importance of how work gets done, not just what work is done, and the expectation of those specific values as the essence of BP's culture were set as the backdrop to the messages.

---

5. *Everyone in*

Well not absolutely everyone because it just isn't realistic to expect you can achieve that. But the point here is to have the mindset and focus to include and invite everyone to take part. You need ownership, buy-in, engagement, activity and energy from the broadest possible constituency of the organization. This will help the pace of change and sustainability.

I have found that in any change, people fall into one of three categories:

- One third of people are enthusiastic, up for the challenge and want to be involved

- One third are unsupportive (noisily or quietly – watch the quiet ones as you may have to work quite hard to spot if or how they are resisting progress), possibly obstructive, often cynical and either waiting to see the change fail or hoping it will (or both)

- One third are sceptically or passively sitting on the fence, waiting to see who will move first and whether they are credible enough to follow.

This is the group that need the most focus as they may indeed be supportive, but under-confident that things will stick, and so wait for others to move first.

It doesn't seem to make a difference to their level of seniority or the part of the business they work in. It's just how people are when it comes to change.

Over time, you'd like to ensure the enthusiastic third are actively involved and even become your informal extended team. The unsupportive third are only ever going to provide limited gains – if you can engage a couple of noisy cynics that's a good result. But if you spend more of your time trying to shift this group, you'll end up focusing a disproportionate amount of your energy on a lost cause. The one third of passive sceptics are a group that really needs attention and over time your goal should be to shift at least half of them (or their sentiment and attitude towards the work) to being more engaged.

It's a bit like a tipping point; you are always pushing something until it reaches a point where it can become self-sustaining. Your passive sceptics are the key to that. If it remains that the enthusiastic third are the only group really active, the work will struggle to become mainstream as the wider organization sees them as the 'usual suspects' in any case. But if you can shift a significant proportion of your passive sceptics then you are likely to reach that tipping point where the work becomes more the norm and less the intervention, where it is truly regarded as an organization-wide priority by more than the change-minded, easily-engaged few.

So be realistic, you won't engage everyone first off, but you do need to ignite the engagement and motivation of the widest possible cut of the organization. It's a key cog to turn.

Seek volunteers. Send out a request for people to get involved, play a part, give their energy, and establish a network through them where you can gather real-time feedback on what's happening across the organization so you know whether any progress is taking hold. On the flipside it provides an opportunity for the wider organization to have their voices heard. A powerful contract of trust can be engendered between you and the network as long as you maintain their anonymity when sharing feedback up the line. Over time, this can create tremendous traction for the change – once that trust is established, you will hear much more of the truth about the culture as you are working to shift it. Of course, you always have to maintain your objective ear, and not get sucked in to solving individual issues, but it's a powerful source of additional insight as well as a way to ignite energy across the organization.

Case Study – Igniting the front line

At BP, we created a Values Network. Over 1300 volunteered and were involved. The membership wasn't established all at once, but grew via word of mouth as well as through formal channels, and it continued to grow over time, as the work became more established and what needed to be done changed. The network was in place for four years. In the first year, as we were working to refine and further define the company's values this provided people with a sense of involvement following the crisis of the Deepwater Horizon accident; a chance for them to shape the future identity of the company and to feel connected to the wider effort to get it back on its feet. A purpose for people, beyond their daily roles. We provided them with:

- opportunities to coordinate input into the shaping of the values
- workshops to engage them more deeply
- training to run sessions themselves in their own parts of the organization and how to effect change with their peers and leaders
- a toolkit of materials to support the aftermath of 'tuning in'.

In years two and three, when the initial noise of the updated cultural expectations had died down and the core task was to ensure the values started to become a reality, we created more formality in the network through:

- carving out a small subset of Values Leaders within the wider volunteer network, given 10 per cent of their time to dedicate to this work, with a formal remit agreed with HR and business leaders, and set into their annual performance objectives. This was put in place for an 18-month period only, to ensure focus
- hosting a regular rhythm of network calls to ensure stories were shared, context was updated and ideas were generated across the network.

The network was in place for four years as a constituency with a mission to reinforce and support change. It was important to formally stand it down:

- to signal the culture was now moving more into 'business as usual'
- to ensure a single, publicised moment to reflect on what it had helped to achieve
- to avert potential perceptions that this work was 'going on forever' and lingering activity was 'distracting' from the day to day operations of the business.

6. *Guiding compass in decision making*

This may seem like an outcome rather than a part of the system shifting, but it is indeed a key input. It's about attitude, and how seriously the culture is taken as part of what really matters.

When doing culture audits to understand the current culture in existence, I ask groups and individuals to share examples of how the values are being lived out today where they work, using real situations of projects and business decisions. In doing this, I am not just trying to understand what culture is displayed, but how importantly the culture is held as a key element of decision making and therefore what really matters.

In nearly all cases, participants talk about the example and then retrofit the values to it, for example: 'When we look at the IT transformation we just completed, it reflects our values of X, Y and Z.'

This indicates to me that the culture, through the values, may be held rather passively. It's a question of fit, not a question of driving decisions. While people may be able to spot alignment, it is not intentional. When it comes to a significant decision, what are the factors that are really driving the decision?

A signal that the system is really starting to ensure that values matter in decision making would be an answer such as: 'We used our values to help inform and plan how we should conduct the IT transformation. We decided against some options because it would not have aligned with our values, what and who we are as a business.'

Achieving this on day one is not possible, and relies on the other five parts of the system shifting too, to help it along the way. But practice makes perfect. It will be a serious test of whether the leadership and the wider organization is prepared to stand behind the culture it says it wants.

Is the organization willing to make different choices as a result of the culture it says it needs to move towards? If it isn't, then either the culture you seek is not the one required, or the one you have is not the one you need. Either way, misalignment exists and needs further focus.

Illustration

Cogs to turn, dials to shift: lining up the whole system behind the culture you need

One clear message	Single definition No changes On repeat
Leadership effort	Individually trying to live the values, honesty about what's hard Focus on embedding into agenda as part of business and personal focus
Policies and processes	Consciously adjust assumptions within formal structures that affect all employees (e.g. recruitment, performance management, recognition)
Symbols, signals and practices	Culture content forms part of the fabric of communications, office environments, the way meetings are run, inclusion networks – the daily rhythm and environment of work
Everyone in	Invite volunteers, give them context, support and missions Focus discretionary effort on the passive sceptics
Guiding compass in decision making	A lens in driving the decision, not simply a retrofit

No single one of these six elements will alone drive that shift in the culture to ensure it is aligned with what it needs to be. Neither will ignoring one of them, or hoping it will work well, be sufficient.

All six need similar effort and focus and treated as an interconnected ecosystem. Because together that is what they form.

Back to the engine analogy. You are trying to tune it to deliver the best performance for the conditions it will face. You may never achieve perfection, and as you tweak one element, another one then needs a little more adjustment.

You could also think of it as plate spinning (more of that in subsequent chapters). If you focus on one part of the engine for too long, then another part moves out of sync and you have to take action to realign it. So balancing the different elements is vital.

And you know you're there when you start seeing the culture being used not just for identity and engagement, but as a guiding compass in decision making (but hold up – you're a long way away from that just yet).

At a glance

Focus on shifting the system first, not tracking the behaviour change

Determine the required thickness of your red thread

There are six dials to turn, and all require equal attention:

1 One clear message
2 Leadership effort
3 Policies and processes
4 Symbols, signals and practices
5 Everyone in (recognising the 1/3, 1/3 ,1/3 reality)
6 Guiding compass in decision making.

Keep focusing on the system to ensure it is lined up.

Don't fall into the trap of seeing quick rapid behaviour change as a sign that new habits have been formed and embedded. They haven't – until the system has shifted for good.

14

Shape-shifting and the life of a chameleon

So we know that 'tuning in' to the culture that is required is only the beginning. And that working towards those expectations requires something much broader and balanced than pulling one lever and hoping it's the silver bullet that aligns the culture.

Remember you are not in control of everyone's behaviour, you are not the one who can or should change everything. You are orchestrating and overseeing the landscape, the system of parameters within which the behavioural shift can occur. The dials need turning across the whole system (covered in Chapter 13). But you cannot sit in glorious isolation with your masterplan and direct people from afar. This requires partnership between you and the wide array of stakeholders across the organization who are going to make it happen. It's only through others that change will take place.

Working well with a wide array of stakeholders is foundational to this work. Not only do you need to engage them, you also need to contract with them and see those contracts through.

In this role you become a chameleon; the ability to hold many forms, and to be able to change them at will.

This role requires expertise in stakeholder management. You will have to shape-shift, adjusting your role, tone, style, channel of communication. You are never one person, you are everywhere and nowhere, always accessible, always responsive. What works with senior leadership is unlikely to work as well with the communications team.

As an air-traffic controller, you are dealing with numerous others and often all at the same time, so you need to be clear on the parameters within which you are working together with each group. Contracting with your key partners is essential. You and they must be clear who's doing what, otherwise either not much will happen, or what happens will be inconsistent and potentially misaligned.

The traits I outlined in Chapter 7 are deployed with all the different groups at various times:

- Passion

- Perception

- Patience

- Pragmatism

- Pedantry

- Pig-headedness.

And don't underestimate how many groupings of stakeholders there are. They aren't simply internal, either.

You are trying to effect a system shift so you will need to work with all parts of that system.

To name a few of your partners:

- Senior leadership

- Culture network

- Process and Function leads

- Communications

- Other networks

- Peers

- Influencers

- Regulators

- Suppliers and Customers.

So now to air-traffic control with your various pilot partners.

Spell it out

Be sure to contract with each of your stakeholder groups. Don't assume everyone knows what their role may be. Far from it, in fact. Never leave it to chance or you will end up with people assuming their role is one thing and you will assume another. Worse still, they may fall into the assumption that you are delivering all the change and therefore they remain passive, pointing the finger when nothing happens. Given everyone owns the work and you are orchestrating the overall approach, you will need to contract with people on their role, and what they are delivering.

The role and relationship is different with each. But the need to be clear with each other on who does what, when, how and a regular rhythm of check-ins, is the same no matter which group.

This can feel awkward and somewhat artificial, particularly with individuals and teams you are already familiar with; but don't skip over it. Clarity up front will save you a lot of chasing later on. This isn't about lengthy documents, or hours of negotiations, it's simply about being clear with each other, and then ensuring there is an agreed schedule to check in and keep track, whether with individual stakeholders or grouped together.

Case Study

When leading the work at BP, I contracted with a number of process and function owners – performance management, ethics, communications, recruitment, talent management and so on. Instead of meeting them individually, it was more efficient for everyone to meet together every six weeks. I would provide latest context on overall progress and challenges around the work, then each individual shared an update on their activity such as a particular adjustment to a process to better reflect the expected culture.

The surprise spin-off effect was that they built off each other's best practice and ideas, and found additional ways to enable a shift in the system through connecting across various processes. Finally, the fact they met as a group meant involvement continued at high levels throughout.

Senior leadership

Plenty has been said in the early part of this book about the work upfront you need to do with the most senior leadership to even get going. But you're not done there, and neither are they. Their role does not stop in the set-up or in the 'tuning in', as reflected in leadership effort being one of the key dials in the system to turn for progress to take place.

On an ongoing basis that effort should be to:

- prioritise, lead for and reward the work

- incorporate culture as a regular part of the agenda in their meetings

- ensure one message, on repeat, no chinks

- work with and engage the wider organization

- reflect personally on their own demonstration of the expected culture not just in their behaviour but in their decision making.

You are in an incredibly privileged position with this group of people. You are the only one to see their vulnerability around the topic of culture and consequently you have a significant responsibility to work not just with challenge and respect but with utmost discretion. You also need to be totally current. They need to be able to trust you. You must have your finger on the pulse of the business – the latest priorities, issues, data, successes, strategic imperatives – as well as the sentiment. They won't have time or patience for you to have to catch up on their issues.

Sentiment and feedback are your areas of specific knowledge that they don't have, so when sharing it don't waffle, use KPIs, examples and stories to back up your viewpoints (they won't accept simply your opinions or your hearsay) all the while holding to the importance of anonymity for anyone in the wider organization who has provided you with honest insight.

Within the senior leadership there is also a split of particular relationships you hold. The CEO is the ultimate owner of the work and therefore your most critical stakeholder within the senior team. But don't only work with them to the exclusion of others. Be mindful of the roles within this team. There may be a specific member of the senior team who is acting on behalf of the team to sponsor the work and spend time with you in between key sessions. There may also be two or three other members of the team who are natural advocates. Think about the role each of them plays and the way you are working with them. Don't be too hard on yourself if you haven't got 100 per cent of the team totally engaged. They are the same as any other audience for change, typically split into thirds of engaged, passive and cynical – just because they are the most senior group does not make them any different in that regard. Work with that smaller group to support them to also nudge and influence their peers in the team. In my experience, you only need three in any team of ten to start making a real shift.

Case Study – Building trust with the senior team

I spent a year working with the management team of a company based in the UK but with sizeable operations in several countries. They wanted to uncover a single set of values that could work across the whole organization, replacing the several different sets operating across the various divisions. The company had refreshed its purpose and strategy and was now looking to line up its culture behind that. I had to work hard to build trust with the team – apart from me not being part of their business and thereby needing to get up to speed fast, the way I was proposing to uncover this set of values was not what they saw as conventional. It required a leap of faith from them that I did know what I was doing. While I was listening to feedback and picking up a sense of the current culture I spent plenty of time listening intently to become conversant not just with the structure but the jargon (and of course the three letter acronyms we all seem to use in business). Being familiar with, and using the language the senior team used was an important element in building the trust. It doesn't help when they have to stop their discussions to explain or translate. The CEO was someone I had worked with before and so we had mutual trust, and the team were clear they were going with it on that basis – the CEO was committed and clear.

However, I was well aware they were somewhat bemused by the process I was running, which seemed to involve so many flip charts, post-it notes, individual homework and not so much around precision and detailed analysis. But over the ensuing sessions, as we merged the feedback from the organization with their views, brought some additional senior managers into the conversation and as we began to hone in on something that they found relevant, stretchy and appropriate for where the company needed to go, the trust continued to build, as did the proactive engagement.

Given the aligned outcome we reached, they were now willing to spend some time as a team assessing where things were. We held the session a couple of months ahead of the 'tuning in' so that they could have a benchmark sense for themselves of where they were starting out from. It also gave them a small runway to be able to front-run the engagement around the expectations and start practising early.

As usual, I gave them individual homework to reflect on: three questions:

   a) where did they think the workforce was strong or weak in terms of the updated values?
   b) where were they as a team against them?
   c) where were they individually against them?

I shared back the collated inputs as an amalgam into the session (no names attached of course), and the result was an agreed set of areas for them to focus on in terms of how they work together on an ongoing basis including their senior team meetings, where to focus the attention with the organization of areas that they were looking to strengthen alignment around culture, and some things to work on personally.

We planned in another session a year later to see how they were doing. They needed time to engage the company on the new values, and to start adjusting the way they were working to align with the culture they are setting as a new expectation. Coming back in three months was not going to help anyone. A year was needed. I gathered further reflection from the organization on how things were going, and asked them the three questions again, individually as homework and then shared back as an amalgamation in the room. The biggest shock for them was that they had considered they had made so much more effort, demonstrated the importance of the updated values, so much more than the organization observed or perceived.

It's a work in progress and will remain so for another cycle at least, in my view.

Culture network

It doesn't matter what you call it, but you definitely need one of these.

It is a set of volunteers who are employees at any level in any part of the organization wanting to take a more active role in bringing the culture to life and ensuring it is embedded as a set of habits and inputs into business decisions. Their role is by no means a full-time job; it is discretionary effort in addition to their everyday role.

Put the call out either before or at the same time as 'tuning in' to ask for volunteers. I'd recommend before – it gives you time to engage them in extra fieldwork as you are researching and testing any update to your culture expectations, as well as support for coordinating the 'tuning in'.

Why?

- The very act of asking anyone and everyone to volunteer to play a part, draws out those for whom belonging to an organization and its future is important in their productivity at work. They see it is more than simply a job.

- It signals that the work is not simply top-down and to be directed and announced from above, establishing a message that this is a bit different and having a voice is part of it.

- Volunteering will create more discretionary energy than being tapped on the shoulder by others, even if it involves the same people in the end. They have chosen to take part, not been asked by management.

Not everyone will get involved in the same way or provide a consistent level of energy or impact. As above, some will simply want to feel more involved and may not contribute much. Don't become obsessed with this, particularly not in the first year. For the very reasons above, it's important to run with who comes forward.

On an ongoing basis their role is to:

- Share stories and best practice

- Hold the mirror up

- Connect the dots

- Contribute constructive energy

- Be agents for organization-wide change.

This is the stakeholder group where you are the leader and have more direct influence than any other. Of course you are not their line manager, as this is a voluntary role they have stepped into where they provide their discretionary energy. But in their role as members of such a network, you provide their direction and boundaries, space and support. This is your group of change agents; those colleagues sitting across the organization who dedicate some of their energy and focus specifically to supporting your mission to shift the system towards the expected culture. As such you define the terms of reference for the network, provide them with toolkits they may request, ensure they have the context they need, provide a focal point for them to share observations, insights, stories and best practice.

They look to you to provide them with confidence that they are doing the right thing, that you have their back, and that you listen. They need to know you are a conduit for them to provide feedback and ideas right up to the top of the organization, but with anonymity preserved. Be honest with them, work hard to ensure you are accessible to them in any way they should choose to communicate with you. Don't be remote, but do be firm on what their role isn't, just as much as what it is. Provide a regular time when you gather them together, by whatever medium and provide updates. Encourage them to share what's not working as well as what is. This isn't a good-news network; this is a change network.

The way you form, engage and lead such a network depends very much on the organization itself. As with all of this culture work, there is never a one-size-fits-all answer: principles, approaches, guidelines; but never a standard recipe.

Think about the different populations across the organization. While you are looking for volunteers, and therefore can't dictate who joins the network, take a look at the constituency that is forming. Is there a good balance between front-line, operational colleagues and more corporate, functional ones? Has any middle management signed-up or is this all the most junior staff who have signed up? Again, there is no absolute right or wrong here, but a network that is skewed heavily to one part of the organization suggests you'll need to do more engagement in another part to encourage at least a few people to get involved.

There is no right answer for how the network meets and works together, other than ensuring there is regular interaction. Don't impose your rhythm or approach on it, but try to mirror the context in which it works.

Case Study

---

a) A financial trading organization was naturally focused on short term deadlines, clear boundaries on decisions and very immediate results. The culture lead's first meeting with the network was deliberately only thirty minutes: fast talking, clear, hard-edged expectations about what the group was and was not; high energy, short sentences, and a promised rhythm of check-ins. No philosophical discussion other than ten minutes for questions. It worked well, playing right into its natural operational context.

b) A customer-focused organization had a wide network of extremely enthusiastic volunteers. They worked best when they sat in a room together in a workshop format for a couple of hours to delve into the subject and their role. They wanted to talk it through, being a group of people whose role is to engage the consumer in conversation.

With others, be absolutely upfront about what the network is and isn't, who is in it and examples of where they are making a difference. Post the remit and the names of members on the organization's intranet, to be overtly transparent. You will face challenge from those who believe the network is a distraction, those who believe you are simply adding activity 'on top of people's already busy jobs' and those who feel threatened because they perceive they are being 'watched' by the network members. In fact there will be myriad stories that circulate about what the network is doing. Many of which will be incorrect or blown out of all proportion. You need a clear and crisp articulation to be able to provide the facts around it.

Case Study – Being very clear about what the role is

I remember when referring to a network once having 800 members, word started spreading that I had somehow added hundreds of people into the organization. Clearly not so; I had added no one; and more to the point, had no authority to for such work. These were all volunteers. I had noted the number of people on the first page of an update on progress, indicating the breadth and reach of the network. In an organization where numbers are a point of familiarity and comfort, this was immediately picked up on as an indication that the work I was leading was running rampant and getting out of control. It was a more sceptical member of a senior team who led with this view. It morphed into hearsay of me having been recruiting people into totally separate roles. Having the remit and the membership transparent for all meant that others quickly did the work for me to ensure people were clear what the network really was and wasn't. The distraction this caused temporarily however, rather than being able to focus the update discussion on the progress being made, was not helpful.

It is a group whose role will evolve over time and you need to be proactive with that. In the early stages it will act more to support engagement, understanding, ownership, as people digest the implications. Then it will need to evolve towards putting the mirror up to colleagues about behaviour, decision making and the general environment.

Case Study

At BP, the network was called the Values & Behaviours (V&B) Network. It originated in 2011 as we were finalising the definition of refreshed purpose, values and associated behaviours.

Everyone was a Values Ambassador. After 12 months we reflected on activity and impact levels across the network, from tracking participation in calls, stories shared, questions asked, engagement workshops run and so on. As we had expected, there was a wide range, from those who were becoming real influencers and those who had signed up and were simply enjoying the sense of belonging.

After eighteen months the organization was truly engaged with the values as the single set of expectations, processes such as performance management were starting to reflect the expectations and communications were consistent. But as with any change of this nature, organizational attention was showing signs of starting to wane, while it was too early to be sure that new cultural habits were truly formed. This was a tricky time; typically the time when senior leadership 'moves on' from the immediate focus, deeming change to have happened.

To work our way through this important time, we adjusted the operating model of the network:

- offered members the opportunity to stand down or re-commit
- defined two forms of membership – Values Leader (10 per cent of time for eighteen months, a formal objective in the individual annual objectives, nominated and signed off by local leadership, more formal change agent responsibility), Values Ambassador (continued informal engagement, storytelling and collaboration role)
- partnered with HR leadership to agree sign-off of Values Leader remit and list of nominated network members from each part of the business
- took the 65 Values Leaders offsite for specific training on facilitation and change management to support their effectiveness.

The regular rhythm of the network updates, publication of membership, gathering of feedback all as one group continued. But the Values Leaders had additional support and responsibility for an eighteen month period. Signalling a specified time period for this more formal role was essential to ensure support for it was secured.

Across that time those individuals were able to more effectively operate in their local environment with some edge. They had the formal backing of the leader in their part of the business and had dedicated time assigned to their role. The second and third year after any major change are the times when new habits are really formed, or old ones re-emerge. So this 'push' was essential to creating the best opportunity to embed the updated cultural expectations.

After the eighteen months, we spent another year with the network purely back as Values Ambassadors, signalling that the network would be retired at the end of that year. By the time it was disbanded it had been in operation nearly four years.

Across the whole network lifecycle, we found that being formal and overt with its evolution and roles helped those in the network keep their energy, motivation and focus. It also provided clear signals to the wider organization that the culture work was not yet complete; thereby addressing one of the biggest risks in this sort work, which is that once the original culture audit is complete, the updated cultural expectations (if required) are finalised and engagement has taken place, 'we're done'.

Process and Function leads

As covered in the last chapter, the extent to which processes are embedded consistently with the expected culture, depends on the operating model. But no matter the extent, functions such as HR, Compliance and Procurement own the processes and policies that are most often applied consistently across the whole organization. It is the leaders of those teams where the processes and policies are designed, who will effect that shift. So partner with them, contracting formally to agree what is shifting, when and how it will be implemented to work into the future.

Their role:

- Ensure assumptions underpinning policies and processes reflect and reinforce the expected culture

- Own design, execution and embedding of any policy and process change.

Agree with the most senior leadership the list of those processes that are consistent across the whole organization that will have the biggest impact both in signalling intent and altering behaviour (See Chapter 13 Red thread). Which ones touch everyone and are supposed to in the same way, which ones are the most visible and front-of-mind for most people in the organization? Target those first. You cannot expect everyone to move everything all at once.

Policies include assumptions that can impact how these expectations come to life. For example, a culture that is trying to drive innovation might do well to instil the opportunity to experiment, to see mistakes as opportunities to learn, and to encourage challenge and idea generation. If signals across the organization, say from the engagement survey, continually suggest that employee voice feels stifled or that speaking up is regarded as risky, then there is some work to do. Taking a look which processes influence what leaders are expected to reward, what is recognised and what not, how leadership behaviour is rewarded, and how mistakes are treated, could help make that shift.

The compliance team owns the hard boundaries of behaviour in any organization, hence another functional partner to work with closely.

Illustration – Adjusting core processes to reflect the expected culture

---

Performance Management	How people behave and apply the values in decision making becomes part of performance, beyond simply what is delivered. It is factored into the overall performance rating for the individual that year, showing that not just what they deliver is important, but how it is delivered, culturally in line with what the organization values.

Recruitment	The values become a lens in interviews and hiring decisions. This does not mean looking for 'clones' but that the applicants can align with and commit to apply the values of the organization in their behaviour and decision making. If they show evidence of personal values that are at odds with the values of the organization, question whether they are going to be able to choose to follow the values of the organization. If not, they may pose a risk to the organization's performance and reputation.
Customer or Supplier Contact	The expected culture is included in the processes and decisions front line staff use in customer/supplier interactions. For example, if Agility is a value, what authority does a customer service representative or the procurement officer have to make a decision for the stakeholder that offers some flexibility and pragmatism around the standard?
Reward	The mechanisms by which people are incentivised can be used to further deepen the sense of what matters. If team performance is to be valued more, then a bigger percentage of reward could be factored off teamwork and less off pure individual achievement.
Recognition	Annual awards, or monthly staff recognition are based off specific criteria. Those criteria can be defined to be particular values or specific behaviours you want to emphasise and celebrate within. A demonstrable celebration of that element to the wider organization is a symbolic confirmation of its importance.
Talent Development	Leadership casts a disproportionately long shadow; who gets developed further and what they espouse as valued will therefore be in the spotlight. Weaving cultural expectations throughout development programmes to reinforce what is sought, and promote accordingly, has huge impact. Those individuals who progress in the organization, recognisable to the broader colleague population as demonstrating that culture, underlines that it matters.
Compliance and Ethics	An embedded culture provides consistent principles around decision making, more than rules, but it has to have edge, and the area of integrity is a hard line, acting as a clear boundary condition for behaviour. Providing an opportunity for individuals to speak up about breaches of behaviour, categorised via the expected cultural priorities, can provide further emphasis that the culture matters.

HR often has the biggest concentration of the processes and policies that we notice and experience directly on a daily basis, whether it is how to embed the cultural expectations in how people are recruited, performance managed, developed or exited.

But don't forget other areas such as workplace environments and whoever is responsible for shaping those. The estates management team will be working to principles for the philosophy, standards and layouts of those spaces and partnering with them to adjust those assumptions for when locations are renovated or new ones are contracted or built, can really serve to reinforce the culture you are seeking to embed. This isn't simply about colours on the wall and posters with the values on it, but about structure and flow of the workspace to instil what you need in how you want people to work.

Case Study – Contracting with process owners

I often start with 'what's in it for me' with a process owner. Everyone wants to make a difference, and having been a functional lead myself, I know the challenge that exists sometimes to truly feel regarded as core to delivering value, especially if you are locationally remote from the operational front line.

Bringing in process owners as part of the coordinated effort to shift the culture is therefore where I start. How can their process, their function be instrumental to progress and join up with a bigger momentum?

It was the same with two instances where I've advised:

- Internal Audit – it's not necessarily the first place to go to help inculcate a voluntary behaviour shift in an organization, but on this occasion there were a couple of leaders in the audit department who were engaged and focused to support the culture shift. We discussed the best way for them in their team to make a difference and landed on using their functional role to do this. We agreed that in each of their audits where they were assessing a whole team, they would include the local culture in their assessment – specifically how the leader was stressing the importance of the expectations, and which, if any, local processes were being updated to reflect them. Through this approach, the importance of culture was formalised within the assessment, the leader received direct feedback on observations and in my role, I gathered another piece of data to assess progress.

- Learning and Development – I was working with a company where there were several third party providers of training sessions. These were all mandatory and the engagement levels of participants was a real challenge. There was some box-ticking for some participants who could not make the connection between their roles, the organization and sitting in these modules. I spent time with the third party trainer for one of the programmes, outlining the background to the culture work ongoing and the targeted goals and objectives to know that progress was being made. She developed a script for each session to set it in this context and agreed it with me. The benefits were twofold: a) participants started to see the relevance of the training in a wider and more connected context: engagement levels rose, and b) I received further data on progress through the insights she fed back after each session from stories heard and questions raised. This helped target other parts of the stakeholder map where it was evident gaps existed.

Communications

Day to day, this team is a close working partner – perhaps your closest. Work together hand in hand, involve them heavily from the start of any culture work. The head of communications works closely with the most senior leadership, so alignment is paramount.

Be careful to really partner with the communications team, rather than confusing your role with theirs. They are the experts in this field, and there is a risk that the culture lead role can present itself as the new face of communications if this working relationship is not managed very carefully and proactively. You need their help, their support. Without it, you are pushing water uphill. Do not inadvertently become a rival, become a partner.

Their role includes:

- setting the organizational tone

- providing the channels for employee stories

- spotting opportunities for reinforcement through hosting the master calendar of events

- amplifying the leadership effort through their regular communications rhythm

- being a vital source of measurement opportunity through employee surveys.

Case Study

I was working with a company that was trying to move its culture from one of recovery, stabilisation and transformation, into one that underpinned growth. The communications team had been working in an environment where the CEO directed them personally around tone, messaging, frequency. Employees received extremely clear updates on deadlines, delivery, requirements; all driving towards restoring performance and thereby trust with external stakeholders. The communications team was on top of its role and remit. However, once trust and performance were restored, employees viewed communication as tactical, top down and not sufficiently engaging. No one felt that information was being deliberately held back; just that they didn't have enough to work with anymore beyond doing the immediate tasks required for business stability.

The communications team, as much as any other stakeholder in the business, needed to shift gear.

They worked together with the culture lead (our air-traffic controller role) to review and adjust their tone and language guidelines, and contracted together to follow it through.

- Messages were to no longer purely focus on delivery dates, compliance and financials, but to be set within a backdrop of growth and cultural expectations.
- All employee meetings which had previously purely been conducted by the CEO were to include more employee voices sharing stories and leading topics.
- The tone was to be more collaborative, language was to be more informal and emotive.

The culture lead asked the culture network for feedback and observations on the updated communications philosophy as well as tracking it themselves. The trait of pedantry was required to help the communications team create new habits and play their part in facilitating a shift in culture over time.

The culture lead did not meet with this team quarterly, but very often daily, particularly in the first year, when the new habits for all needed to be established.

Other networks

Inclusion networks are often filled with members who want to be involved in the organization to a greater extent than simply doing their job, and who have particular passion about a specific focus. As a result, they can be highly engaged groups who will also be change agents, in addition to the culture network. Rather than asking them to be huge advocates for the desired culture, help them apply the culture to advance their mission. For example, rather than asking the Working Parents network to simply advocate the values, work with them to identify the values they could most effectively deploy to influence awareness and internal policy on the topic they are focused upon – Working Parents. Make it about their mission, not about yours: you'll get more traction with them and in doing so, you are helping to apply the values, not simply engage around them.

Peers

Not a formal group of people, but colleagues who can quietly be so influential with and for you. Who is it that you really talk with, who do you know who can move things, who others listen to or look to? Your peers are both your secret agents and your release valves. Are there any of your peers who are in the one-third group of passive sceptics? If so, work hard with them to see if you can engage them in a specific task. It could pay huge dividends to overall momentum. You don't need many to move, a few impactful leaders can make a massive difference. Given your more informal relationship with your peers, if you've known or worked with them a while, the opportunity to have a different conversation with them is there. Use it. Be aware that this goes both ways and should do – ask them to put a mirror up to you as well, not just about sentiment in the organization but observations on how well you are executing your role also. It's never harder to hear than from peers, but it's never more valuable. It is done informally and can help you course-correct while on the go, without others noticing.

Influencers

The negative way to look at this is it's a bit like herding cats; because influencers by their very name are those who people choose to follow or mimic and you'd like to know what they're up to. Their behaviour and actions have an amplifying effect, so if they are off track it's one heck of a job trying to corral them into some sort of direction you really need. The other way to look at it is as a real opportunity. Being an optimist, I choose the latter.

In Chapter 7, I shared a rule of thumb of one third of people being supportive and engaged, one third negative and one third stuck in the middle in a mix of passivity and scepticism, and how this final group is where some real impact can be found if done smartly.

There are some marvellous influencers within this group; those who people really listen to, look to for signals of what they should follow, and act as bell-weathers for organizational sentiment. If you can work one or two of these individuals into an engaged partnership position with you in this work then you can make significant progress. Imagine the impact of working with three of these if there are twenty-five other people influenced by each one – that's seventy-five people engaged, who otherwise would not have been. It's a healthy return.

Case Study

I first met Cliff, fellow long-term BP employee, a shift leader and union convenor at Forties Pipeline System, a BP operation in Scotland, when I was conducting a first set of focus groups on a working session in Aberdeen in 2011. It's one of those moments you never forget. He sat down next to me, highly engaged and at the same time noisily sceptical about the session. He didn't say much until everyone else had spoken. I asked him for his thoughts since he'd been so quiet and he asked how honest I wanted him to be – I replied 'both barrels please'. I remember comments shared with verve about 'suits from head office in London', 'another corporate initiative that is today's favourite flavour', and most memorably 'we'll see you once and never again. That'll be you off down the road again tomorrow and that'll be that'.

In that moment I decided I would confound his expectations. We had a lot in common: he clearly wanted more for the company, was proud to be part of it and needed his voice to be heard more loudly. He had bundles to offer – energy, experience, expertise, and was more influential than he perhaps realised.

I asked him to stay back after the session and talked more, I asked him to get more involved and I promised him I'd be back. I followed up with him individually, invited him to working sessions in the 'head office'; and yes, I went back, a number of times. I worked hard on it; I was determined for him to be an active partner in this, not a noisy critic. We got on. He equally followed through, throwing himself into active participation and as a result bringing others right at the operational frontline with him. I knew this involved him putting his reputation on the line as well, with his frontline colleagues. He was one of the first people to volunteer for the Values & Behaviours Network (what we called BP's culture network), one of its most active and long term participants. In the end, he became a de facto extended member of the team conducting sessions in partnership at other operational sites and also on his own as a Values Ambassador and later on, Values Leader. I remember one particular time when we decided to run a workshop together at our chemicals plant in Hull: D Shift. Cliff being there, the way he delivered messages, the clear partnership and trust between us, made all the difference with the team on site. We averted the sort of reception I'd had first time in Aberdeen when he and I had met, about the 'head office' perception, by him being there from the heart of the operations. Cliff was the ultimate litmus test for how ideas would land in the operational community; never one to hold back on feedback or different solutions, he constantly put the mirror up to ensure all our work was seen from the point of view of the wider organization.

We remain very much in touch. We listened to each other and built mutual trust and respect. Cliff could have been the noisiest of critics, but was the biggest advocate of all for how to understand, shift and manage a culture, and the business imperative of such work.

Regulators

If you are in a sector where there is one, your relationship with a regulator may be simply as part of a wider sector context or it may be as a result of some specific regime your organization is under. In either case, treat this group as a stakeholder to engage with proactively. Not only are you providing them with assurance of where your culture can be moving towards, but they may be able to provide you with examples from others in your sector or across different industries of what others are doing. If nothing else, you are likely to gain additional ideas. So often, regulators can be viewed as 'the enemy' but I have found that they are more likely to be looking to find the best examples of what they are seeking to inculcate; so adopt a mindset of working with them, rather than trying to avoid them at all cost. Don't assume they are always trying to find fault.

The very fact that you are proactively engaging with them gives them a signal that you are working on the culture, and in the context of increasing regulation around organizational culture, that in itself is a positive message you are sending.

Case Study

At one organization, having conducted a culture audit, then presented it back to the board, the senior management team and the organization, the CEO asked me to then join him as he reported the findings back to the regulator. This wasn't because they were under formal monitoring, any more than other companies in their sector. It was all about trust and transparency. The company had experienced an operational crisis a few years before and had been focusing on stabilising and building back its reputation, within a sector that had been under additional scrutiny by the regulators. The CEO was comfortable with me sharing all the findings – the good and the not so good. This openness was received extremely favourably by the regulators; another step back in the company's external rehabilitation. On the other side, the topic of culture was one the regulators were starting to be more vocal about and so this acted also as a valuable opportunity for them to test out their theories and experiment a little with a willing participant.

A win-win for both parties.

Suppliers and customers

Too often culture is held as purely about the internal ways of working in an organization, and that brand is the piece on the outside. Well yes and no. While it's important not to confuse culture and brand, they do overlap because the way you work inside has direct impact on the external stakeholders you touch every day. Don't ignore suppliers and customers as you are trying to align the culture you have with the culture you need. They are the ultimate test and measure for what is happening right at the coalface.

Try to find a couple of strategically important customers and suppliers as well as a couple of one-off or more infrequent stakeholders. Speak to them both as you start out understanding the culture today, and then later on once the culture is under way to embedding. A balance will give you a sense of both what happens when the company knows the relationship is truly important, and during the 'when no one's looking' interaction. It's important to be able to see if there is a difference: a helpful area to test when you are tracking progress to see quite how deeply the culture is embedded.

And as with regulators, it's a strong signal of being listened to and regarded with respect if you are making the effort to understand how they experience your culture. That can only stand you in good stead.

Shape-shifting

Stakeholder	Their role	Your role
Senior leadership	*Sponsors* of the work *Decision-makers* on definition of the desired culture *Iconic role models* of leading for and rewarding the expectations	Trusted advisor, confidante, critical friend, ears to the organization, occasional stick-wielder
Culture network	*Agents for organizational-wide change* through stories, best practice, connectivity, holding the mirror up Constructive *energy contributors*	Set direction, boundaries, space and support Crisp clear articulation to others of the network role, activity and impact

		Proactively manage role at different stages of change
		Provide confidence and a focus point for questions
Process and Function leads	The *engineers of infiltration*, by driving expectations into processes by which the organization operates. They design and deliver the embedding	Set expectations for inclusion of content in the process
		Track effectiveness of implementation
		Essential source of data
		Do NOT design or deliver the process change
Communications	*Organizational tone-setters* Channels for employee voice and leadership effort Spot opportunities via master events calendar Measurement via employee surveys	Working partner; particularly close on 'tuning in' Provide the frame and content for emphasis and repetition Agree strategy around different media for messaging and stakeholders
Other networks	*Early adopters* of the desired culture to further their network mission	Equip them to apply the culture. Focus on their mission not yours.
Peers	*Secret agents of influence* by role modelling and incorporating the expectations with no formal programme role *Your emotional safety valve*	Ask for help and feedback Test ideas informally
Influencers	*Fuel injection* to wider engagement of the one third passive sceptics group	Provide a targeted-few with additional data, ideas, opportunities to shine
Regulators	*Benchmarkers* or *Auditors* (depending on your context) to the outside world – reputationally influential	Provide assurance through examples of efforts, evidence of learning and search for improvement
Suppliers and customers	*Bellweather, market sentiment*	Ask for feedback on progress

Many hats

As well as being clear on the different roles you are playing with various stakeholders, you'll need to be able to switch seamlessly. On any one day you may be working with several different stakeholder groups at different times, so being clear on which role you play with each of them is important. Flipping between these styles can only be done effectively if you really have spent some time thinking about it upfront, not just yourself, but with them.

It's basic, but try to find a few minutes between each meeting or interaction to be able to take one hat off and put another one on.

I was queueing at the immigration desks at George Bush International Airport in Houston a few years ago, waiting to get through passport control after landing. A man in another line was, literally, I kid you not, wearing three fedora hats, one on top of each other. He was stopped at the line for a long time. I have never forgotten the image. I don't know whether he did it because it was simpler to carry them like that, or because he had forgotten to take some of them off as they were so light. In any case, don't be that man. Try to be conscious which hat you are wearing and only wear one at a time.

Backroom omnipresence

While wearing your many hats is a juggling act that requires conscious thought, remember you need to find a balance between being omnipresent in your accessibility and not running the show out front. With all these stakeholders to manage and the effort you invest in wearing those hats, it's all too easy to occasionally fall into the trap of showing up like you're controlling everthing.

Two things are going wrong here:

- You are not controlling everything; you are coordinating, facilitating, nudging, shoving and cajoling

- People will subconsciously abrogate their responsibility to play their part, if you leave them with the impression you are 'running things'.

It's a delicate balance and one that is difficult to get absolutely right. You may find yourself always slightly too much on the control side or slightly too much on the support-only side, depending on your stakeholders and how far along you are on the shift. That's ok, it's not about precision; it is aboutbeing alert to it and adjusting accordingly. Ask for feedback from those very stakeholders.

Always on show

Having just said it's important to find the balance between control and support, it may seem contradictory to now stress that in this role you are always on show. That's just the same as any other role, but for this sort of work, where there are so many sceptics as well as those looking to be further engaged, your impact is so much about influence.

It means your demeanour (and that includes your body language and your facial expressions), your focus, your energy are all signals you are sending about how the work is going and its level of importance. You are the lifeblood of the work for as long as it takes to become a new set of habits. You are not simply coordinating: you are very much orchestrating and that involves a heap of informal influence. Recognise the significance of your brand as part and parcel of the long term success of this work.

At a glance

You are clear on the dials that need turning, but it's not your role to turn them.

The widest array of stakeholders deliver the goals, not you – you set the parameters for the whole system.

Define the different groups you must work with.

Contract with them on your role, their role, and delivery.

Keep in close touch providing context, and joining them up with each other.

Hold them to the agreements; see it through.

Learn to switch hats at a fast pace because you'll be working with many different groups each day.

Find the balance between control and support.

Remember you're the ultimate bellweather of the work until it's embedded.

15

Like a stuck record

The culture you need is now clear.

The organization has tuned into it.

You are under way with orchestrating the expectations being woven through the fabric of the organization.

The leading indicators are starting to bear some fruit; not all of them, but you can start to see the shoots of hope. The dials are moving.

The culture network is active.

The senior team has been focusing regularly on this topic for a while.

Can we let the pressure up a little now?

Actually no.

The time to continue to be boringly consistent is now. Fight any sense of 'job done' from inside your head or from others, and remember that while you must continue to present that passionate and energized tone about the work and its progress, you must continue to put the mirror up to that progress, shining a bright spotlight as you do, into all the nooks and crannies that will show you that your job, the organization's and the senior leadership's is far from done.

You've reached the end of the beginning.

Push on; it'll be worth it. As with any new habit that is forming, it needs repetition far longer than we expect, for it to really have stuck and become a new normal.

Channelling your inner pessimist

Your energy and passion for the work is required to support momentum, whether that is belief in its criticality or pulling out stories and measures of change to underpin confidence that things are moving forward.

But at the same time you need to hold a sense of inner pessimism. This may seem a real conflict, given that passion is one of the core traits I outline as essential for the role, but it's an important tension to hold.

While pushing forward, always be on the lookout for the weakest link, any gaps you spot, any leading indicators that tell you something is not embedded, messages are inconsistent, priorities are not aligned. This doesn't mean you should be announcing these, but going directly to the source to find ways to overcome them, and basing your myopia about sticking at it and keeping the pressure up and focus on, off those signals; not off the most positive ones.

Remember as the person leading the work, you are the one with the best view of the overall system, whereas others will have their own narrower snapshot and so may only see the positive progress. Some may only choose to see the negatives of course – the noisy sceptics – but they are always on the lookout for evidence to prove their point.

Be hyper-honest with yourself and err on the side of caution.

A slow grapevine

It's amazing how rumours and hearsay spread like wildfire to all corners of the organization at an alarming speed. Yet, the opposite seems to be true for anything that is a new and formal expectation, and certainly one that is seeking to override or replace something that is already in place, that people are familiar with.

It isn't just the old adage of people taking seven to ten times to be given a message before they truly receive it, this is about how long a traditional cascade process takes to reach the entire organization, and how ineffective it can be, especially if traditional top-down methods of communication are applied.

Too often, by the time the expectations are properly rolled out to the widest reaches and right to the front line, the leadership at the centre has already moved onto another set of expectations. And that doesn't even take account of the inevitable imperfections of people not quite following the cascade approach to the letter.

It isn't therefore simply enough for messages to remain consistent, for formal retirement of old ones to take place or to find ways to ignite the whole of the organization at once rather than relying on cascade; it's also vital to stay on message and to become bored with the sound of your own and the wider leadership's voice on the updated expectations, and to be consistently vigilant for gaps and wobbles.

Case Study

At BP, we experienced the realities of how much time a traditional cascade process can take before messages can be received and implemented at the front line of the organization. When we were carrying out our inventory of the material that was still held as being in operation, (even though it had been superseded by other material in the meantime), we found examples of parts of the business only three months earlier having run a full workshop rollout of a specific leadership framework that had been formally launched in the company two-and-a-half years earlier.

The issue was not the commitment of the local leadership, the blockage had been the cascade process along with a host of other items from central teams and the local leadership wanting to schedule rollouts in at regular intervals to ensure the organization did not become overwhelmed.

Old habits die hard

Like with any habit, it takes a long time of consistently forming a new habit before you can say the old one is now no longer in play. How many times, when trying to break a habit have you done really well in the early stages, then let up the pressure only soon to find yourself back where you started? Mostly it's because the new habit hadn't had time enough to bed in. It hadn't yet become the new norm because enough time had not passed, enough cycles of the same tricky and key situations had not come around again.

Forever and a day

When is this critical period of required repetition and consistent focus; how do you gauge how much longer it should last? Referring back to the four stages of competence (Chapter 9), it's the phase when trying to move the organization from conscious incompetence into conscious competence, and keeping it there for a while, so moving from 'Hitting the Pain Barrier' to 'Practising Hard'.

A useful guide might be to look at the critical time between the first and second cycles of processes and events. You may have updated the performance management process; doing that once means the process has been changed, but doesn't mean there are new habits in place. It's very rare for a process to be improved or a system to be rebooted and for it to work perfectly first off, or for the users to be working within it seamlessly from day one. It's exactly the same with embedding a shift in culture.

But do not be lulled into a false sense of security, subscribing to the belief that you have got it right the first time! You need to be ready to have to take a look and hone for two or three cycles, before the environment has aligned with where you need to be.

Case Study

At BP, we had updated the entire performance management process concurrently with re-defining the desired culture. As a result we were able to underpin the 'tuning in' of the new expectations with a single global structure that covered both what individuals delivered and how they delivered it. Behaviours (the how), as specified within each defined value, were now to become a formal part of an individual's performance rating.

In that first year, engagement, training and further communications were shared across the entire organization to outline the updated system. As well as including job description and the objectives for the year, each employee now had to pick at least three of the twenty-five behaviours (five behaviours associated with each value) that would require emphasis to ensure the objectives were delivered. The key here was to tie the behaviours to the day to day business objectives – not to see them as personal development.

We were able, through the systems to analyse the percentage of employees who had picked each of the behaviours, which later down the line we used as an effective piece of proxy measurement as to where the organization believed behavioural focus needed to reside to deliver the business priorities.

But in this first year, it quickly became apparent that while in principle individuals had embraced being measured on how they do their job as well as the deliverables, there were significant pockets of the organization that had continued to follow their own definition of effective behaviours and values; not the company's updated definition. We found several thousand responses that included behaviours not related to the ones the company had laid out only a few months earlier. In some cases we found this as isolated cases, but more often we found the same behaviours cropping up time and time again which revealed that team leaders in some locations had created their own behaviours to target and had issued an expectation of their team to include them in their performance objectives.

So the principle was established, but that was only half the requirement. We needed everyone to follow the **same** set of behaviours and values.

Seems simple, but in retrospect, we should have seen it coming. Even though the form had stated that the behaviours to be referenced were those from the company framework, unless we made it unavoidable, humans would be humans, and choose to 'improve' the set to be more 'locally applicable'.

In the second year, we created a drop-down menu on the form online, so that there was no opportunity to write in behaviours in free text, but only an option to choose at least three of the twenty-five company-wide ones. In Year 2, therefore, we started to see compliance with the content, not just the principle.

But it took till Year 3 before we could see the tipping point reached where there was real compliance to the principles and to the content, and finally performance calibration discussions really digging into people's behavioural delivery as well as activity delivery in an active way. The ultimate signal was when some individual's performance ratings for the year were adjusted up or down as a result.

Enough is enough

A mark of success here is to be told by others that you are indeed like a stuck record and that you are becoming boring and repetitive on the subject.

A second one is to observe colleagues challenging others, particularly their peers and those more senior than them, on the use of or accuracy of the expectations. When people are calling out others because they don't see them using the right words, or not talking about the expectations at all, then you know things are starting to stick.

If they can also articulate back to you accurately just what it is that they expect you to say, not just the content of the expectations, but how they are to be used, then you are starting to see signals that:

- expectations really have been heard

- messages are not changing

- they may even start to matter.

That's when you begin to know you may be able to think about easing up a little on the constant repetition. The organization is sitting more comfortably now in the Practising Hard phase and parts of it may even be heading into the Sunny Uplands.

But ease off slowly, and if you see things slide, resume the boring repetition.

At a glance

Put your glass-half-empty hat on and assume there are weaknesses and gaps even where you can't see them.

Be prepared to focus on the consistent messaging, process updates and regular rhythm of the air-traffic control for a lot longer than you initially expect:

- This particular grapevine is slow.
- Old habits die hard.

Two or three process cycles after 'tuning in' is not a bad proxy to follow:

- It's not just compliance with the principle, but with the content, and then making it really matter.

Only when people predict (accurately) what you're about to stay, and you can see examples of processes being aligned towards the culture without you asking for it, then might you think about starting to ease up a little.

16

Filling buckets not spreadsheets

In your role, by this stage you will have your own 'sniff test' of how things are going. But for good order you do need a consistent method and some sort of framework. Being really clear on what it is you are measuring and for what reason is important for continuing the trust you are building in this work. It's also important for you, so you don't end up off track by being sucked too deeply into a particular aspect.

The persistent challenge from others as to 'how do you measure culture' will be ringing in your ears as you conduct this work. A seemingly straightforward question turns out to require some structured thought.

- Do you simply measure how people are behaving?

- Or are you monitoring your actions and interventions designed to effect change?

- How are you tracking how the system is changing to ensure culture alignment has the best chance?

- Do you need to construct a precise scorecard with financial metrics, or go purely for something qualitative?

- How often you do measure progress?

And why does it matter so much to spend time thinking about measurement?

Apart from the obvious – being clear on your measurement approach is vital to ensure you keep on track, build credibility with others and are able to make adjustments along the way – it is also a form of risk management. Sceptics and cynics can turn the measurement discussion toxic with comments such as 'you can't measure it', or 'tell me the return on investment'. You need a clear answer and approach, and, as ever, making sure you keep it simple and consistent.

Similarly there are those who will expect you to measure absolutely everything. This could lead you down the road of spending all your time tracking data rather than focusing on effecting change. It's impossible to do so with precision and you are fooling yourself if you follow this route, wasting your time buried under dashboards when you could be doing more air-traffic control on the change that is the end goal.

Take some time to be clear on your measurement strategy.

That requires thinking about not just what you measure and why, but when you measure it and the processes and data you use to provide the most effective illustration of progress.

This chapter outlines what to measure and how to measure it, for the time that you are trying to embed your culture, through four lenses:

- Leading over Lagging – focus most of your measurement on how the system is shifting (see Chapter 13) rather than whether behaviour is changing (that becomes more important later on).

- Proxy over Precision – find measures that indicate signals to you rather than only looking for precise answers, which may be few and far between, as well as potentially misleading.

- Exploration over Invention – there is plenty of data already available to you in existing channels that can provide you with signals; don't assume you need to create new structures. In fact, shy away from new structures as it creates new work.

- Finding and plugging leaks – think of what you are measuring as a set of buckets you are trying to fill. Remember they may have leaks at the bottom, so be alert to them and work hard to plug them or you will make little sustainable progress.

Leading over lagging

It is all too tempting to jump straight to measuring behaviour, habits and perceptions once you have 'tuned in' to your cultural expectations and you are working hard to shift the system within which everyone works.

But don't.

When you take your car for a service, all the different elements of the engine are tested first – the diagnostics – to test all the elements that create the overall performance. Engineers don't jump straight to measuring the sound of the engine or its fuel efficiency. They check oil levels, wheel balance, condition of the tyres and brake pads, engine tuning and so on. All the elements of the system. The leading indicators for performance.

Just as your air-traffic control activity is focused on adjusting the various elements of the system to make it somewhat inevitable that the actual culture becomes the expected one, then so should your measurement be.

I am not proposing that you completely ignore the culture you want to see: of course not. Finding those great examples of the values coming to life through people's behaviour and the business decisions that are being influenced by the values, should be searched for and then celebrated. This gives confidence and recognition to those who are working in this way, provides tangible examples to others of what the culture coming to life looks like, and ensures a consistency of message to all around the expected culture. It also provides the most senior team with tangibility around the work, particularly important for those amongst them who remain a little sceptical about focusing only on the system.

But as you are working hard to embed the culture you are now expecting, the focus of your measurement should be on the system – the diagnostics in the car service.

And remember, as per the previous chapter (Chapter 16, Like a stuck record) you will need to stay here for much longer than you think.

Over time your focus will need to shift to a greater balance on tracking the culture itself, but never to the total exclusion of the system. Think of the lights on your car dashboard that occasionally come on in between services, providing an indication of areas where you'll need to do a bit of repair or intervention. It's the same with culture.

Once you are into a more steady state, then that's a different focus – (see Chapter 17). It will be much more of a balance between checking the system is still aligned and effective to support the culture you need, and the culture that is actually playing out. But don't assume the system, once aligned, is then stable. People join as others leave and need an induction on the expected culture, awareness levels dip if messages are never reinforced but assumed, processes are tweaked over time and can move out of alignment if not checked intermittently. But it won't be as intense as in the two to three cycles after you have tuned into the updated expectations when the spotlight is bright and the workload is particularly heavy on the system and forming new habits.

Proxy over precision

There will be pressure on you to use metrics that show precision in progress. But culture work is about direction and alignment, not about precision. I think of it as asymptotic – in Greek meaning 'not falling together' – the distance between a curve and a line that approaches zero at infinity: that's to say you will never get to your desired culture with precision. You can't.

It's the total sum of people's behaviours, interactions, perceptions – none of which are precision, so how could you measure with precision? And the context in which people are operating is constantly shifting: it doesn't stand still, so neither will people's behaviour. But you can certainly approach the culture you need.

Your true measurement is the ability to provide signals, symbols and pieces of data that demonstrate an overall picture of a system and thereby a culture moving towards what you need it to be. Some of it can be quantitative, but providing data that shows precisely how many of your actions you have completed is not going to provide any clarity on whether the work is making progress. It is purely reflecting your activity.

Sometimes it's the stories that seem tangential to the focus that are the best signals. They can appear to be minor items, but they are sometimes the most accurate reflections of the deeper dynamics.

Case Study

I return to the example I used in Chapter 7, but to make a different point. I was visiting an operational site recently with a colleague. This particular piece of business had been a joint venture (JV) until a few months prior, when it became a wholly-owned entity. As a JV there had been two company brands both equally visible on all signage across the site.

As we separately parked in our visitors' parking space, we both got out of our cars pointing at the parking signs. After six months, they all still showed the two different brands.

This may seem a small signal, but it was the very first image we saw of the operation, and any visitor would see. It told us that we should be on alert as to how the leadership was ensuring that the whole operation was culturally integrated. It also told us that none of the employees were either noticing this or had been listened to. Neither were great early indications.

And unfortunately, this proved to be a very true signal. Once inside, it was clear things weren't right at all. The leader was not engaged in the importance of cultural integration to ensure the best performance, but merely to keep tracking to the timetable. Sickness absence was up, there had been a few minor safety incidents in recent weeks, and the site just wasn't operating as it could or should. Needless to say, action was taken in the aftermath. But this simple signal of the sign in the car park had actually provided us with a powerful proxy for what was really going on.

Exploration over invention

Don't create extra work for others when you are trying to measure progress on culture. It won't help your engagement efforts and it really isn't necessary.

Proxy indicators, using data that is already in the system and checking for alignment between what is expected, what is really happening and who is really making the decisions (and how), will give you a sense of depth of change.

Tap into existing processes and data sources and try to avoid adding additional lines or initiatives of measurement. It will slow you down when you are designing them and it will be an additional burden in the system to others. Instead, piggy-back onto what is already in action through the regular rhythm of the business.

Practical examples of using existing measurement processes	
Employee Survey	Make sure questions get into the employee engagement survey each year, don't create your own survey: are there five or six questions that you could track consistently across three to five years to monitor progress on understanding and engagement in the expected culture, observations on it coming to life, belief in it being part of how business is done.
Internal Audit	As the internal audit team reviews parts of the business or specific processes, include questions on culture in their enquiry: what formal cultural expectations are expressed in the business or embedded in the process?
Induction	When graduates are being asked after induction what their experience has been, ask them to comment on visibility of the cultural expectations in their interview as well as their induction; and how the current culture compares to what is laid out as expected.

Remember, what you are trying to do is not just shift the culture, but to establish culture as a core element of strategy and performance, not something separate, so drawing out data from existing processes rather than setting up new data-gathering streams, reinforces that.

Focus not fixation

Measurement is an important part of building credibility around the work itself, not just the progress it is enabling. There can be a tendency to over-measure, in the hope that the more data you gather and display, the more the sceptics will trust the work, get on board and continue to commit. But be careful. First of all, more metrics doesn't necessarily tell you a lot more. I have found that five to seven from different parts of the operation can start to create a representative picture.

Secondly, as the old saying goes, 'a pig doesn't get fat just because you weigh it every day'. My point here is that you need to spend most of your time working to coordinate and orchestrate the change you are trying to enable not just tracking its progress. Being visible and present in the organization, working to support and nudge stakeholders to make progress and thinking up new strategies to be able to keep ahead of the curve are all where the focus of your time should be spent. Yes, you need to measure. But not so that you are doing more measuring than actually orchestrating. As is becoming a mantra as you read this book, there is no specific amount of your time that is the right amount for you to spend on measurement, that's up to you to find the balance. But think of that pig when you're ploughing through your sixty-five metrics to prove your point.

Case Study

When I was first leading this sort of work, someone in a programme office, more senior than me had decided I needed some additional external consultancy help to focus on performance management. As I think back, this was a classic signal that credibility was still weak for this work as there was a fixation on being able to provide a structured set of KPIs far more than there was on change actually taking place. I was given a full-time person for this, and told that this cost would not come out of my budget; the resource would simply be provided. This was fairly ironic, given I only had one other person working with me to coordinate all the work and my budget was minuscule in any case.

But I challenged back that I only needed them for about 20 per cent of the time. When this was not accepted as sensible, I decided it was not a battle I was going to win, so simply accepted the additional resource gracefully and focused 20 per cent of her time on performance management, which involved both her ideas on where we might find data in existing processes and translating the raw data we were pulling into something that illustrated themes and insights. For the other 80 per cent of the time she partnered up as a member of the team working on engagement, storytelling and mapping where we were with different stakeholders.

She had brought with her the thirty-two different items to track in order to check that progress was being made – we used five. If we had followed the thirty-two, probably more than 50 per cent of my time would have been spent collecting and reporting data against the thirty-two elements, rather than working to shift the system. We both laugh about it now, seven years on. We are still working together, just in very different guises.

Finding and plugging leaks

I visualise the elements of the system that need to shift (as in Chapter 13), as a set of buckets. What data can you find that tells you those buckets are filling up over time? And what tells you that a leak in the bottom is slowing down progress? For all the great progress that is being made, if there are factors that are undermining it, then those are the leaks and for the work to make a lasting difference and the organization to truly form new habits, they need to be plugged.

Weak signals on data can provide you with a sense of whether there are leaks in the bucket and how seriously those leaks are undermining your efforts to fill the buckets. Look out for them when you are investigating your data. We are all on the lookout for quick wins and the positive signals that we can share and celebrate to provide confidence and credibility; but look for the weak signals that tell you some things are still not lining up.

Examples might include:

- Number of internal audits showing parts of the organization defining their own standalone culture different from the organization-wide one.

- Group functions continuing to create behavioural frameworks separate to the values and saying they'll tie them back in.

- Your culture network providing feedback that their leaders are talking publicly about the work being only an initiative.

Case Study – Example measurement dashboard

Shifting the system	Filling buckets	Spotting leaks	Sources of data
One clear message	Consistency of words across all channels and to all stakeholders	# parts of the business creating their own separate or additional expected culture # incidences of retired material still appearing on any communication material (internal or external)	Internal audit reviews as part of regular reviews of parts of the business
Leadership effort	# requests for help from individual leaders	# times culture is bumped off the top team agenda	Culture network feedback from team meetings, conferences
Policies and processes	# performance appraisals and objectives forms including values or the associated behaviours # individual performance ratings upgrades/downgrades as a result of values (or associated behaviours) displayed # processes touching all employees that have been formally updated to incorporate expected culture as per agreed plan	# values or behaviours referenced that are not those outlined Exit interview data reflecting an experience at odds with the expected culture	HR existing performance and pay review meetings HR recruitment and induction marketing and decision making material Internal Audit

Shifting the system	Filling buckets	Spotting leaks	Sources of data
	Feedback from new hires that the expected culture formed part of their hiring process		
Symbols, signals and practices	# senior leader speeches referring to expected culture, or referencing specific values # work environments changed (as scheduled) to incorporate values	Speeches revert to purely the 'what'	Communications team and speech writers Property services
Everyone in	# culture network members (initial, to track engagement) % of culture network active e.g. attending culture network calls, sharing stories, asking for help	% employees regarding this as an initiative	Employee survey Culture network
Guiding compass in decision making	Feedback from strategic client on specific deal/working relationship	Exit interview feedback where culture regarded as 'lip service'	Key customer feedback

Familiarity breeds comfort not contempt

While measuring a culture shift is not a precise science, those you are engaging (especially senior leadership) are looking for tangible results and often by KPIs. They want to see trends that reflect progress, and while you may be tracking signals day-in and day-out, others are not. So give them consistency in what you are tracking to ensure they can get into the subject fast again and see at a glance whether things are on track or not, without having to re-educate themselves each time as to what the overall level of progress is or isn't.

Given some of your KPIs will be proxy measures and some will be qualitative rather than quantitative, it is vital to create confidence and assurance with your stakeholders that what you are measuring is representative, and part of that is to provide consistency. Don't stop others adding examples in (in fact it may be a signal that they themselves are becoming more competent in this area and really starting to own the work); but be sure to have a consistent format and some measures that are seen every time over a long period.

While your activity set may chop and change and you need to be a chameleon, this does not hold true for measurement. Be boringly predictable with your tracking; create familiarity. It breeds trust.

Measurement and meaning

Given KPIs can be challenging to define for progress on a shift in culture, it is all too tempting to add in anything that indeed can be measured precisely as a signal that the culture now matters and that it is being lived out.

But be careful.

Some signals are not necessarily telling you what you first observe. Be discerning and really challenge yourself whether to take it on face value, or indeed to apply a slightly different interpretation to it. Think about the context of the data you are seeing.

Take the number of cases reported through whistleblowing or compliance and ethics processes in the few months directly after a major engagement on culture. Fantastic, I hear you cry; that's definitely going to be a KPI on my dashboard, providing data as to how people are incorporating the values into the way they work, and whether leaders are supporting or blocking it. Surely the rise in cases reported shows that values are being taken seriously; and doesn't it also prove our analysis that there is a gap today between the values in action and the expected culture? What a great baseline for the future to track:

if the number of cases start to decrease then that gives us evidence of behaviour 'improving' (aligning to the expected culture).

Not necessarily so.

It could be; but more often this is simply due to increased understanding of cultural expectations due to the engagement. The clear communication of behaviour expected from everyone, and the emphasis on its importance gives title to particular issues that individuals may have been experiencing and a yardstick by which to measure how wrong it is. They log a complaint that a particular leader or peer is behaving against value X.

It doesn't necessarily mean the behaviour has become worse recently – possibly simply that the individual who is experiencing it now knows that it contravenes the expected culture and that it isn't to be tolerated. Over time, as the number of reported cases reduces, similarly it does not necessarily mean that there are fewer cases of mis-aligned values – it may be that it is a long time since anyone has reiterated the expectations (so they are no longer so front of mind for some) or the processes by which complaints are raised.

Every situation is different; I am not trying to generalise. My point is to take a second look at possible data sources and investigate what signals they are really sending. It may not be as simple as the headline.

At a glance

Pick apart what 'measuring culture' means

Plan your strategy in advance

Five important principles:

- Leading over lagging
- Proxy over precision
- Exploration over invention
- Focus not fixation
- Finding and plugging leaks.

Create your format and stick with it – keep it simple and consistent so others get used to it and recognise it.

Don't simply take the data as a KPI because it's being measured; think hard about what it is really telling you; keep asking yourself 'why?'

PART FOUR

GETTING TO THE OTHER SIDE

17

Aren't we done yet?

No matter what anyone tells you at the start, senior leadership's attention span on culture can be short. We all know that, whether we are in that group or not. Context always changes, unexpected challenges arise and different priorities emerge. And there may be some still in the camp of 'it's just a fix that needs to be achieved' (you'll never capture everyone's full ownership – be realistic). Be ready for the top team to want to move on once the desired culture has been defined and tuned into. They might think that now there is a tangible product and your approach is sound, then people will quickly adopt it in their work. You have to find ways to keep the work on their agenda throughout the time it takes to instil the change. As already outlined in this book, it will often take as much as three cycles after the new culture is defined; and getting the dates in the diary throughout the process is key; not just for the early stages.

And it isn't simply senior leadership you face this challenge with. All the stakeholders will have some sort of change fatigue long before the shift has started to become a set of reinforced or new habits. They may see progress or a radical change in their own purview. The messages may start to feel repetitive and maybe even a bit tired. But you are the only one who has the full picture of progress, given your air-traffic control role and how you have approached the work, and will hold the true picture of where the organization sits (whether it's Sunny Uplands, or still stuck in Practising Hard – see Chapter 9).

Remember while you may see gaps, weaknesses and inconsistencies, the vast majority of your partners in this work only see pieces of the overall jigsaw, including the effort they have put in, and may see progress more optimistically than is really the case.

Freshen up

As you continue to have the regular rhythm of progress updates with the senior management, think hard about adjusting a number of elements, to keep things interesting.

There is a balance to be had between consistency (same risks, same map of change, same format of material) and holding their interest by mixing things up and moving them on.

While in the first year or two you might need to spend time with them on a high frequency, as the work moves to a different stage in progress, adjust the frequency downwards, so that you have more chunky progress to share with them each time. You might have been having a monthly session, move it to a quarterly one, but change it around so that rather than you updating you are asking them to reflect on where they believe progress is, what examples they see and where they might need help.

As the work moves from simply embedding the expectations in the system to new habits and behaviours forming as a result, then what you are measuring must also shift. Over time, shift the balance from sharing all the data on the ways in which the dials in the system are lining up (one set of words, leadership making the effort, the processes being updated) and increase the focus on examples of new habits and behaviours in action, business decisions that were influenced by the desired culture, the impact of the updated expectations woven through the processes.

As well as providing new angles for discussion, it will continue to build confidence that progress is being made (which of course, it is).

Mix it up in terms of how the updates happen. Use video stories, bring others into the session to do the talking instead of you (your culture network is ideal here), plan with one of the senior team that they do the update not you.

In short, think creatively, think pragmatically and above all be proactive in keeping one step ahead of the senior team's impending topic fatigue, to keep them on their toes, interested, thinking, challenged and, surprising as it may seem, recognised by you when you've seen or heard of them doing something in this area that is making a difference.

Calling time

A focus on culture should never be wound up completely. As I reinforce across this book, shifting a culture is not a one-off project but a time when there is an increased focus and effort, followed by returning to the regular embedded rhythm of tracking, reflection and adjustment to ensure things remain aligned – just like you would with strategy.

But, as you reach a stage where you're heading towards the Sunny Uplands, that you have been practising for a good while and you have the data to show you that new habits really are forming, then it is time to step back from that intense focus and go into more maintenance mode.

Find a way for it to be you, the person coordinating the work, who calls time on it being a regular agenda item in its current state, on the senior leadership agenda. People are far more disposed towards you and your work if it is you, not them, who has worked it through to a sensible position and then said you don't need quite so much time with them. Try to plan it a good few months ahead of time. This gives you time to set expectations about how it will work into the future as well as plan an impactful final deep dive session with the team reflecting on where you started, and where the organization is now; and to plan ahead on communications with the culture network and other stakeholders about how things are shifting.

But make sure it's you who sets that agenda – hence another reason to plan it well ahead.

But not really . . .

Remember, what you're calling time on is a regular set of updates in some sort of programme mode with the senior team, or formal meetings with your culture network or processes owners. But you are not calling time on the focus towards a desired culture, or culture being an ongoing part of the operational focus generally.

Even when you are not 'running' the work anymore, your 'calling time' means you know that the legacy of the work continues in the form of:

- organizational culture embedded into the senior team's ongoing operation

- others taking on the mantle of this work day to day because it has become part of how they run their teams and conduct their business

- someone being the guardian of the content of expectations to ensure consistency.

But this doesn't just happen. It involves you working with some of your key stakeholders (peers, culture network, process owners, business leads) to set up that legacy well before you have stepped away from the day to day focus of your air-traffic control work.

In the process of calling time with the senior team, ask them why they believe it is the right time now to do so. Look for their understanding of what progress really looks like, whether processes are now reflecting and reinforcing the expectations, what their ongoing cultural focus now is as a team, and how the organization is working more effectively as a result of the work. If they can't answer, other than to say they have other priorities, I would propose that you don't quite call time, and take them back to the remit, the definition of success you all worked together, and the risks you agreed such as 'declaring victory too early'. It won't be comfortable, but you have a responsibility to the wider organization as well as to yourself, not to compromise now as you're reaching the goals you aimed for.

Case Study

At BP, in 2012, the work had already run for two full years when, during September, as the executive diary was being finalised for the following year, there was an assumption that the regular sessions would no longer be required at the executive meetings.

For the senior leadership they had spent one year defining the required culture, one year signing off progress updates as the expectations were woven through organization-wide procedures, and had been supported and challenged by the Values & Behaviour Network. They had spent a year since 'tuning in' talking with others, practising and improving their own behaviours and decision making, and observed that projects other than this work that were also contributing to the company's recovery, were finishing up as projects. So from what they experienced, they saw that the work therefore was reaching maturity and no longer required such regular updates. It was to be re-classified as moving into steady state from the following January; an ongoing part of how the company was going about its business.

Yet this was the very moment, two years into the work, when follow-through and repetition were required. The processes had been updated with the expectations, but there were still improvements to be made in the next cycle around usage, impact and being able to track whether different decisions were now being made. Each process, such as performance management, takes three cycles to become a new way of working beyond simply an initiative.

There was an added hurdle of projects that had been put in place following the crisis coming to conclusion and this created a general sense that such intense focus was no longer required.

I talked at length with the executive sponsor, providing examples from the measurement work of continuing weak signals as well as reflecting back on the top risks we had identified (e.g. declaring victory too early).

I remember him telling me he was shocked because I was normally such an optimist, and that if I was expressing a concern that more needed to be done, then it was something to be taken seriously. And the data didn't lie. And the stories were compelling.

I worked hard to negotiate an extra six months of regular updates at the meetings.

He had become such a working partner by this stage he agreed we'd simply add a whole year. He talked with the CEO and for the following year I appeared at the senior management team meeting once a quarter.

At a glance – Keeping senior leadership attention

Accept that senior leadership attention span on this work may be shorter than yours.

Balance consistency of focus with freshening up the way you share progress.

Think ahead to adjust your frequency, measurement and media for updates, to hold others' interest and guard against topic fatigue.

Drop it as a headline and weave it into other titled work i.e. embedded examples.

Ask them to define why they believe it is embedded and how the way the company works and makes decisions have changed.

18

What we really meant was . . .

By the time the work has been in progress for a number of months or years, either fatigue may be setting in ('are we still talking about this; I thought we were done') or self-congratulation by those who commissioned the work in the first place may be the tone of any reflection.

And this can set in when only the earlier stages in any change have been achieved: the start of awareness, understanding and engagement with that expected culture.

This could be through the values being part of everyday language, or with employee survey results showing that recall of the values is improving and line managers are making the culture a focus of discussions and team meetings.

Such progress is absolutely necessary, and don't underestimate the importance of getting to that stage. But it is not sufficient to be able to say that the refreshed culture is now fully embedded and 'just the way it is around here'.

The expected culture must form more than a sense of identity and engagement for it to become the new norm and to underpin and enable further strategy and performance delivery. The real proof that it is taking hold is when everyone knows that by using the ethos, principles and expectations of the updated culture, different decisions may need to be made. In those moments, what happens?

It's the real test.

It's not enough for everyone to believe that the work environment has improved and the way people behave in their interactions is more aligned with the expected culture. It also needs to matter as part of the business that is done.

But this is one of the toughest steps in any work on culture; when it comes to the difficult moments, are we really going to follow through on what we say is important about the culture we need as this organization? Is it truly how we do business; are we willing to stand behind it and use it as one of the core principles for a decision, or do we only want to go as far as the work environment and how we'd like to behave with each other? When it comes down to it, is it a theoretical utopia but one that in reality we know we'll back away from fully implementing, when things become too hard or uncomfortable?

One of two things happen over time here, if it is held as the latter – theoretical utopia:

- The expected culture will become something to be mocked and regarded with cynicism, because the business decisions may act at odds with it. When it comes down to it, everyone knows how it really works and what really matters.

- Alternatively, if it is held so dearly by employees that it is the way the organization should do its business, and yet it isn't, then people will leave, or drive the culture underground and act against the prevailing norms of decision making.

We are back to alignment yet again.

In any event, customers, suppliers and other stakeholders will be provided with a confusing message, and employees experience double standards.

For the culture to matter, it can and very often will create uncomfortable tensions. But all too easily people will slip back into trying to find compromise and avoid those tensions. This could be because it involves difficult people conversations, or it could be a sign that they have yet to buy into the culture truly mattering as part of the ongoing purpose and strategy.

It will happen, whether it's only one person at the top pushing back or more of a systemic challenge; and you need to be on the lookout for the tell-tale signs.

Don't assume the work has failed at this point. It hasn't, because you are ready for it and you won't let that happen. But if you allow compromises and retreats on decision making in these formative years of the updated cultural expectations, without calling it out at the very least either it will take a lot longer to reach alignment, or it may not make it at all.

While it is important to have tested these sorts of scenarios when defining the culture you are seeking, there is no substitute for the real life situation and I would advise you to be realistic that this sort of pushback will happen.

When there is a decision to be made about a piece of business that is not in alignment with the expected culture, this is the time you need to push back, stand up, call it out – and have others do the same. If the top leadership is wobbling, the organization will notice. People look to their leaders to provide

Tell-tale comments you should expect

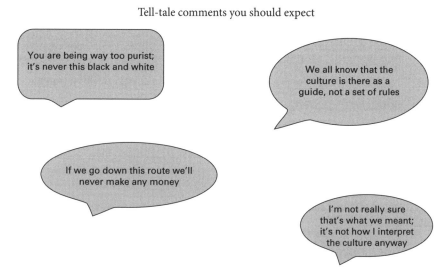

FIGURE 18.1

signals that the values matter, to provide confidence that they too can and should use the values as part of the decision-making process.

Be sure to call on a couple of the key traits for your role here – pig-headedness, patience and passion – a mix of all three are required here to be able to help make this work matter. It's a critical moment in whether it really does come down from being words on the wall and into everyday work.

I am not suggesting that there is ever a fix-all solution, but there are plenty of things you can do to try to address this.

With the senior team, if you are in this situation:

- Take them back to presentations and discussions from earlier in the process when they were working to define the culture required and why. They started this work because either they had a crisis and therefore absolutely need to be making different decisions, or because they sensed there was misalignment and it was resulting in less than optimum outcomes. Challenge them to reflect on this and ask them why they think they will achieve different results if they are unwilling to change their decision making. Show them the material that was their work, their diagnosis, their summary of what needed to change. Sometimes it's simply a case of needing a reminder. Other times it may not be so straightforward and 'the context has changed' will come back at you.

- Find some customer, supplier or partner feedback that shows how they value the stand your organization is taking on a particular issue that reflects your updated desired culture (it could be operational, commercial, risk-based, political). This may have emerged as part of your work in diagnosing your current and defining your required culture. External stakeholder feedback is extremely impactful – in fact often more so than the team's own views. If there is a customer who is promising to do more business with the organization as a result of the updated set of cultural expectations being used to inform decision making, then that is a powerful incentive for the most senior decision makers to further reinforce such expectations.

- Empathise with them, signalling that this is difficult, that they are not the first team to experience this. It could be that as individuals they don't feel confident that their colleagues will use the new cultural expectations as a factor in decision making and they therefore do not want to risk putting their own neck on the line for this work in case they lose face. So it may not be belief, but perception of other's attitudes. I have seen it particularly to be the case across more middle levels of leadership. Give them examples from across the organization showing the resulting impact (a balanced scorecard of outcomes here). Allay some fears with them by working through some theoretical examples. I have found that a focus on embedding the culture through the system to impact decision making and being true to the expected culture can be perceived by some to assume dogmatism and extremism. Partner with them to show you mean pragmatism and consistency. It is a seemingly subtle, but a big difference. For example, if you have a value of focusing on safety, and a definition that includes never walking by and shutting things down if you aren't comfortable with them, does that mean you would then shut everything down as it's an inherently risky operation? No, of course it doesn't. It means that you are managing risk, not there to remove it altogether (or you wouldn't be in the business in the first place). But this may need clarification. In effect, test the boundaries with them by working through some examples. It will help bring things to life and avert some of the potential to avoid using the new culture at all as it seems too idealistic.

With the wider organization:

- Your regular check-ins with your culture network provide you with a temperature check of how much retrospective expectation setting is going on, how much compromise is happening. Ask them to share these stories when you are connecting as a group, so that they come to the surface early on and regularly. There is no point in pretending they don't exist. The earlier you recognise them, the earlier you can together learn how to deal with them. This is so often a feature of the conscious competence phase, where the organization is really practising how to use these updated cultural expectations and quite how far, therefore, to push it.

- Ask your most recent and junior intake, such as graduates or interns, how they are using the values to help them make decisions. Given their limited experience inside the organization and quite often within this whole environment, they are quite likely to have the freshest eyes and the least cynicism about 'we've seen this all before'. Work with them to understand what is practical and what use of the cultural expectations would ensure they stay with the organization and what sorts of compromises on their use would start signalling to them they should leave. Ask them to practise using the values within their daily decision making to encourage others.

- Talk to your peers: find out where their confidence levels are and how they are working with the expectations. Sometimes the best examples are found in the most hidden places in the organization. The individuals who are leading these teams can be powerful catalysts for others to see that the expectations do indeed matter beyond the daily work environment. Similarly, watch out for their tone: the most connected ones create a significant ripple effect and if they are talking about the cultural expectations simply being a rough guide and supportive rather than influential, then this can have a dampening effect for the whole organization. Work with them 1:1. Give them a chance to be a hero in their own environment by suggesting examples and practical suggestions of how they can achieve better results by taking the expectations seriously as part of decision making.

At a glance

A truly embedded culture goes beyond engagement and identity (though they are the necessary foundations).

It must matter as part of business decision making and this will create tensions – if it doesn't, then nothing is changing.

When it gets hard, retrospective redefinition and compromise may well set in.

With the senior team: revisit commitments, share stakeholder feedback, empathise for pragmatism.

With the wider organization: work through the culture network and junior new hires to surface it early and raise expectations from the bottom up, work 1:1 with peers to bolster confidence.

Create peer pressure to make it matter, not to water it down.

19

Once the adrenalin rush subsides

Managing a shift in culture, whether it's to align today's reality with what's already expected, or whether it's to shift today's expectations into a freshly defined set, has a certain adrenalin rush about it. Even through the hard yards of coordinating and embedding the shift, it has a whiff of change, progress, improvement and dare I say (as I only use the 'f' word with extreme caution when it comes to culture), fixing something that wasn't quite right.

But I opened this book with a reference to culture being as important as strategy, not simply as an intervention but as an ongoing guide for making decisions every day. While all the good work you will have done means that the new habits required are being formed, as with anything, a complete removal of focus and guidance will result in a lapse in consistency over time. Old habits will re-emerge or new habits from other sources are imported via the inevitable churn of people into and out of the organization.

So how do you manage culture once the adrenalin rush has gone, once you have moved into the 'Sunny Uplands' area of the culture focus; when there's no great cause for disruption or need to mobilise the organization to engage behind a refreshed direction?

How do you keep it ticking over? Like a ship leaving port and being set on course, what do you need to do the make sure it keeps going in the right direction? It may not need the heavy lifting of the initial preparation and departure, but the weather could change, the engines need monitoring and maintaining, other craft may cross your path – if it's not always the captain, someone always has the overall responsibility of the duty manager and keeping watch.

You need to move from protagonist to custodian.

And remember, you need to treat culture as you would strategy: you've had your strategy refresh, you've adjusted the system to ensure it's working towards that strategy, now it's about tracking its delivery, and checking in annually to ensure things are on track.

But how do you make this move, how do things run once you've done that and what should you watch out for in the process?

Protagonist to custodian

So much of the work of leading a culture shift relies on a focus on yourself and the role(s) you are playing at any one time. Yes, you are trying to engineer a system shift and as a result, habit and behaviour change from hundreds or thousands of people in aggregate. It's their behaviour that is in focus. But yours, as the lead, has a critical impact on the work which in turn shifts the dial one way or the other, and never more so in the latter stages of embedding.

I have found this work is as much an exercise in self-discipline and management as it is in organizational change.

By the time you have been leading the work for two or three years, you really will be in flow, master of your culture universe, and now comes the hardest of times – easing off, stepping back, letting go.

Again, a common theme through this book, you will need to think ahead of where the current level of progress is, and plan how to adjust your role from being the person who has been the agitator, fixer, master change-agent, air-traffic controller, trusted ear, to someone who is seen as the expert, wise counsel, observer, commentator, quiet steward.

Becoming less proactive and more reflective.

Knowing when and learning how to take a step back to enable the organization to fully own the desired culture, takes thought and careful planning.

Move too early and inconsistency and misalignment creep back in. Being your own pessimist on where progress really is means that you need to stay in agitator mode longer than you at first imagine.

Move too late and you could become entrenched, unhelpful and flip over into 'being in charge' (remember, you never were, you were coordinating; but with teeth not gums).

I am not suggesting that there is a perfect time, to the day, when you adjust your role, but to be conscious that it needs to be done, and that it sends a big signal to others about the status of the change. Don't just let it happen, plan it, and ensure it is formally announced, with context. Check back to where you think the system really is (still Practising Hard, or Sunny Uplands?) before you move.

This involves moving your role from being in charge of the coordination of the work to stepping back and ceding 'control' to the organization. Shift to become the custodian of the culture, the observer, the expert on the topic, but not the air-traffic controller any more. You may need to be ready to be called in for a shift now and then, to unravel a few lumps and bumps when someone has 'gone rogue'; for example when someone has taken it upon themselves to adjust the cultural expectations to 'better fit their local needs'. In these cases work behind the scenes; fire up your Internal Audit pals and the people who were in your culture network to raise a flag and sort out the local situations themselves. But more often you will be taking stock of where things are, and remaining the beady-eye overseeing overall progress.

Think of it as a driving instructor who has been running dual controls with their pupil as they learn how to drive from scratch. You now know they are competent enough to drive unaided, but they have not yet taken their test and so are still officially learning. You are still there sitting beside them, on hand to take over the controls if something goes wrong, but until it does, you're the expert passenger. The pupil knows you are there, but doesn't need to call on you.

Calling time on the current form of your role is hard. But oh, so necessary, at the right time.

Setting up the next stage requires some planning and formality. Don't just let it drift into its new form.

You may have had a small team of colleagues around you who now need redeploying, to carry on their culture focus within other roles. There will be stakeholders to re-contract with about what you do and don't do into the future e.g. the senior team and your working sessions with them. As you adjust your role, each of the relationships you have with stakeholders should be shifted, not by chance, but purposefully.

And it needs a communication to the wider organization. The shift in your role is not the headline in itself but as part of a broader message that outlines how far the organization has moved towards aligning today's with the desired culture and the continued importance of this as just the way the organization works.

Such a signal provides reflection and recognition back to everyone that they together have moved the dial, and that it is therefore only logical that as they have shifted the system and formed new habits, there is no longer the requirement for you to keep your foot on the pedal. It is owned by everyone.

Equally, however, stressing that your role moves to custodian, shows that culture is not now 'done'. It would be helpful to outline in that communication what your role does now involve. It gives you a calling card and it lets everyone else know this isn't just a polite way of saying 'we're done'.

From protagonist to custodian – the shift in your role

	From	To
	Air-Traffic Controller	Sage Expert (Master Shifu)
Culture definition	Guide the process to uncover and finalise the content of the desired culture. Enforcing its consistency	Ownership authority/host for the content
Culture network	Lead the rhythm of activity with formal network of culture change agents	Check in occasionally with former culture network members Be there for support when asked
Senior Leadership	Private working sessions, putting the mirror up, providing active support, regular rhythm of progress updates at management meetings	Annual review of progress On-hand for quiet advice Known to be monitoring embedding at a distance
Process and Function leads	Contract with leads on format and timing of adjustments Provide regular context and receive progress updates	Using data to continue insights on progression of culture shift

Monitoring culture on an ongoing basis – treating it as you would strategy

The custodian role sits at senior management level	• Reports into, or is a member of, the management team • Scans the horizon to ensure fit and responsiveness to changing external conditions • Is the custodian of holding to the direction and expectations • Ensures the articulation remains consistent, clear and measurable
An integral part of the CEO and their team's operating rhythm	• Annual review of progress and fit • Medium/long term plan reviewed and refreshed every few years • Included within annual performance objectives of the top team • Ongoing tactical decisions must fit within the expectations

It's publicly declared as a short-hand for how to make sense of how the organization aims to be successful	• Internal channels • External where relevant, such as an annual report
Across the organization	• Someone has responsibility for the local application • Maintain its inclusion as part of the employee value proposition for recruitment, engagement, performance management, development, retention

Get over yourself

Having coordinated the work to this stage, where you have moved into a custodian role, you will feel proud and more than a little pleased with yourself. And quite right too. It's been exhilarating, exhausting, frustrating, hugely satisfying, and taken all the passion, perception, patience, pragmatism, pedantry, pig-headedness you could muster, over an extended time period.

Surely now is the time you receive the organization-wide plaudits, the thanks, the eternal gratitude that somehow, you managed to do something that others just couldn't work out a way to succeed in. Isn't this your moment in the sun? After all, you deserve it don't you?

No, this should not happen, not if the work has been truly successful.

If the organization wants to put you in the spotlight, that is a signal that it doesn't yet own it fully. If it does want to do this, push back, hard as it will be. Don't ever reject a quiet compliment and private recognition from those you have worked with closely. Privately, that's a different matter; those who you worked with closely know this is your legacy. But don't let yourself be paraded as the culture hero, no matter quite how tempting that really is.

If the organization really now is operating towards the desired culture, culture is seen as core to performance and the work you have led and coordinated has been successful in that sense, you will need to find a way to reconcile yourself with your part in that never being fully recognised publicly.

The best measure of the success that the actual culture is really aligning with the desired culture is when the organization believes 'this is just how it works around here'. The change is not seen as a project imposed on the workforce, instead viewed as a set of tools and an environment that supports people to do their jobs better; a workplace they choose to participate and thrive in. If they are new into the organization they see it as part of its fabric, its DNA. If they are already here, then it's become the tribal mantra they are working to – and it belongs to everyone.

Your finest reward should be to know that 'it's just the way it is', and no one really knows quite how it happened.

If you need more tangible closure than this, write a book instead: I can guarantee, it's deeply therapeutic.

At a glance

Success doesn't mean everything stops. It's time to move into maintenance mode.

Your role now moves from protagonist to custodian.

Do it consciously, purposefully and with plenty of communication to all stakeholders – don't 'drift off'; formalise the change. It's a big signal in itself.

Others' role now shifts too and there's some recontracting to do.

True success means others assume the shift evolved naturally and the culture (and the ongoing focus on it) is simply the norm (or even their idea!).

Accept you won't get the credit – get over yourself and quietly know what you've achieved, with pride.

20

Stepping away and back (though possibly read this at the very start)

A test of endurance

The true test of the focus on culture is not that it makes a big splash in the short term but that it endures. There are two parts to this:

- The culture becomes a more important part of the ongoing business agenda, beyond an intervention.

- The content of the culture that you are trying to engender remains intact until any change in strategy.

It takes time for new habits to be formed; whether it is purely to put culture more at the forefront of decision making or for the specific behavioural aspects of that required culture to be borne out systemically. In my experience, it's three to five years before you can see a sustained, recognisable shift. Given it takes two to three cycles to line up the system through tweaking all those dials of communications, processes, symbols, language, it would be optimistic to presume the actual behaviour has reached a tipping point whereby this is the new norm, in anything under three to five years.

Take a look at companies in real crisis – it's a good three to five years before they are objectively considered to recover (if they survive, that is) and then can be up to eight years before they learn to really grow again. It's similar with managing a culture to a new norm (a sustainable new norm, not simply a seasonal fad) as it's all part and parcel of the same shift.

Culture within culture

An organization with a strong culture has a common red thread running through it of what it means to belong to that organization and what it truly values.

But no organization is a mono-culture. It is not a set of clones, all thinking and behaving exactly the same way. Even in those organizations where the operating model means the culture is highly consistent throughout a deep set of processes (a red rope rather than a red thread) people are individuals and different.

Organizations today are increasingly global in their constituency or at the very least in their outlook, just by the very nature of the way people communicate and run their lives, as well as their market places.

In your air-traffic control role you will need to take account of how a more global employee group and also wider stakeholders, will interpret cultural expectations as well as how change happens in different geographies. A word in one language may have different connotations when translated into another language. How people are motivated and what makes them tick across different cultures needs careful consideration and respect. How you work with your stakeholder groups to get things done will look very different in different geographies.

Working with a leadership team that is global versus one that is all from a single geographical culture, requires more time in explanation as well as far more intentional and active listening, to overcome assumptions.

Case Study

We had spent a long time not just working to define the different values at BP but how they worked together. Would they provide sufficient tension, would they work together well as a system to underpin where BP needs to head, as well as deepening the existing cultural strengths?

We looked at the definitions of the words in different languages and how nuances may shift the interpretations as well as the length of the words in different languages, purely from a formatting angle (*safety* in Polish is quite a long word).

But it was only when we started engaging further on them beyond the 'tuning in' as they were starting to be operational in the organization that real discussions across geographical boundaries emerged as to how they really worked.

In Singapore, we were running a workshop to engage people on what the five values really meant and how together they represented the system of attitude and behaviour. There were quizzical looks and a few frowns amongst our local colleagues. When we asked how people would work to apply the values, it was clear that two of them – Courage and Respect – were causing some discomfort and confusion. For some in the room, their understanding of the Western meaning of Courage was one of constant challenge, proactively standing up to authority. For them, it stood in direct contravention of Respect.

To our rescue came the five behaviours that defined each value.

When we dug into them, discussed them and the sorts of situations they could apply to, everyone agreed that Courage, through these five behaviours, could complement Respect and was not a de facto undermining of authority.

Even though we had deeply considered different meanings of words in different languages, and used the behaviours to define them in as full a way as we could, we had failed to recognise the assumptions that different cultures make about what other cultures really mean by a word.

But it's not only geographies that form cultures within cultures.

Different job families can form different sub-cultures within any organization. An engineering firm is not only populated by engineers – accountants, marketers, sales staff, receptionists, all work for the same company. Don't under-estimate the potential for them to form their own sub-cultures. They will and they do.

When doing the BP work, motivating a set of marketeers in Castrol in the UK was a very different set of workshops than spending time with drillers and engineers from the BP business in that same country. Engaging business developers in Indonesia took a different approach to working with oil traders in Singapore.

Organizational heritage is another element to be very conscious of. When companies merge or acquire other companies, employees are thrown together in a new identity. While data shows that the number of organizations we work for and the career-types we have are increasing in numbers across our working lives, there are still millions of people who have worked for one organization for a number of decades, and they have become very used to the sense of belonging within that organization and the 'way of doing things around here'. When one company buys another, the unwritten rules of them both are not immediately obvious to others. This can cause a real sense of confusion, loss of identity and lack of engagement amongst those who have been 'acquired'. Surface the informal parts of these cultures and decide whether they are to be incorporated or replaced. Don't allow them to fester or ignore them. Tread carefully if you are aiming to replace. I'd advise not to, in fact, especially if this involves a significant number of people. The company was acquired for a reason, which includes how they approached their business, so why would you ignore or quash that?

Generational differences need to be taken into account when working on culture. The more hierarchical models of mid-twentieth century business management are giving way to flatter approaches that recognise choice and engagement. As a result, there can be strong differences between the way generations react to and engage with culture work, with those more used to the hierarchical approach of 'command and control' reacting more sceptically to culture work that is focused on a pull (not a push) approach of trying to understand what makes others tick and to engage them.

I have found that constant enquiry is essential. Not every society raises its hand when it is uncomfortable with something, so you need to enquire. Curiosity is a vital ingredient in this role. No one geographic, job family, organizational heritage or generational culture is right, but the culture you are expecting needs to be understandable and applicable in that environment. Don't push ahead without taking real stock of this. Recognise you will have your own subconscious biases and assumptions from the business environment you have grown up in. Back to behavioural economics again – while everyone may have access to what seems like the same data, we are still likely to make different choices due to our unique contexts and ambitions.

I have become so much more aware of my Western business assumptions, my behavioural economics approach to business and my BP 'mother-tongue' of business culture since starting to work in this area. It's simplistic to say one culture is like this, and another like that. They aren't. The critical factor is to recognise there are some trends, traits and backgrounds that impact us, and to recognise that. In doing so, it helps you recognise that others have the same, and they are different from you. Don't assume. Enquire. Listen. Understand. Go to where the organization is, go to where individuals and small groups are, not where you are.

Crisis drives candour

I am conscious, looking back, that the conditions under which real reflection on a culture take place do influence the candour with which people generally, and particularly the most senior leaders, share their views.

It was only when I took stock a couple of years later, that I realised the first year after the major crisis at BP in 2010 was a time that was rich for this work. In the first few months after the accident the most senior leaders were incredibly open to looking in the mirror, spending time on real reflection in a manner I had never experienced in my previous twenty years. No subject was too sensitive to discuss. The agenda was about saving the company and ensuring a stable footing as soon as possible. Every topic was on the table, nothing was off-limits. After a few months, I had to work harder to draw people out, as the immediate crisis evolved into a longer-term company plan and rehabilitation. I had had to seize the moment while we were all most open to it. The difference here was that the whole senior team was facing the same context, the company in crisis. When the situation is less extreme, and more about continuous improvement, or re-setting the strategy to capture more growth in the medium term, the challenge is that often the CEO and the Head of Strategy and a couple of others may be very open to exploring without boundaries, but others in the team may not be, given their context may be slightly different. When the context is as black and white as a crisis, it can drive more candour due to everyone starting on the same page as to the outcome.

Choose alignment over satisfaction

I have often heard people refer to a culture as strong and healthy when what they are really referring to is an enjoyable working environment. That in itself is an important factor, but it isn't sufficient. And in some cases it may not be the primary concern. That sounds a bit like heresy. But it's quite like employee surveys asking about satisfaction rather than engagement. Everyone being deliriously happy about their work environment may be fantastic for retention, but unless it has purpose it may not be productive or even taking the business in right direction to deliver its strategy. If you have a strategy to disrupt the market, then everyone being very comfortable may not be enough. What you need is a culture that is driving invention, breaking a few eggs, bristling with energy and ideas.

If you have a turnaround strategy to urgently drive the business away from crisis then you need a culture that is about discretionary energy, going the extra mile, following the leader over the next hill because they have a plan.

What is vital here is alignment, not simply a 'great' culture. One is about workplace satisfaction the other is about underpinning and helping to drive business strategy delivery.

Of course, they are not mutually exclusive. Both are required – it is not possible to sustain a culture where everyone is miserable. But be sure to recognise the limitations of workplace satisfaction without a set of values that are driving business decision making.

Work with what you have to shift it

This may sound counter-intuitive, but unless you want or need to wrench the organization completely, then some of the most effective ways to shift elements of your culture may be to use current traits within it. For example, if you have a strong culture of networking, then use that approach to get the messages out. Go with a more viral approach, encourage people to form groups to create engagement, share ideas and ensure stories are shared.

If you have a culture of innovation, then ask people to come together to think of the most innovative ways to 'tune in' to the culture.

Of course, your goal is to ensure that the misaligned or unhelpful parts of the culture are diminished, so don't try to use those ones to shift things. But there are strong elements in your culture you will no doubt want and need to keep, and even enhance, so use them to also propagate the culture you seek.

Don't dismiss the politics of an organization as dangerous or obstructive by default. Understand them, why they exist and what they might be working to achieve, and you may be able to use them to further the shift you need. Influential individuals can have disproportionate impact – you just need to work to get them pointed in the direction you need them to be. Herd those cats.

It's all a balancing act

I have never found myself perfectly content with how I am showing up at any time doing this sort work. And that is the challenge, in my view; recognising that you are always going to need to nudge a bit more, hold back a bit more, be firmer, step back for a while, pile in and intervene, or stand back and be invisible for a while. Managing culture, whether to shift it or on an ongoing basis, is a dynamic situation. Know that you are juggling not perfecting, influencing not instructing, and you will get more done. Don't beat yourself up when you realise you have either been pushing too hard and alienating a few people or letting things become a little too stable. The trick is knowing where to look for the signals that tell you that you are the wrong the side of the line at any one time and being able and willing to adjust your own activity and demeanour to move. That's not to say it isn't sometimes highly frustrating and often unsettling, to know that you will rarely be spot on. Find yourself a good confidante who can provide you with some reassurance.

Worse before better

Don't be surprised if the tone seems to deteriorate as the focus on culture increases. This can be hugely disheartening, and cause a serious wobble, especially amongst those who are sceptical in the first place. It doesn't follow that it automatically will feel worse, but I have found that it is often the case.

Why?

Because this is now a topic that has been given permission to be aired. Feedback is being actively sought and expectations around culture are being woven into the process fabric of the organization. Everything around culture has more spotlight on it. As a result, you may find that issues lying under the surface previously are brought to the fore as they now have a 'home'.

It is now much clearer what is acceptable and unacceptable, so again, cases that may have been debated or brushed under the carpet as 'just the way it is around here' are targeted and more formally dealt with. A concerted effort to tune the organization into the desired culture drives a sense of expectation that things will be better, clearer, more formalized and they are more likely to be vocally disappointed or discontented if situations don't alter immediately.

No finger-pointing

People's behaviour, the way they make decisions, who they network with, the tone they set, the long-held biases they exhibit, the sceptics and cynics – it can all be extremely emotive. But avoid finger-pointing at all costs, and ensure there is someone you trust who will point it out to you if you start to do it. First of all, accept the culture you have today. It is what it is; don't try to pretend it isn't there, and don't blame others for how it is or how far away it is from what is required. I started this book referring to behavioural economics and the importance of recognising that everyone has slightly different contexts (ambitions, backgrounds, experience, skills, outlooks on life and so on). Because someone's regular way of working is now different from the required expectation does not make them wrong, or bad, or a blocker at the outset. They may have been rewarded for that behaviour over the last ten years, or had to work that way in order to cope with a difficult boss, or could have been in a part of the organization that has just been taken over and their whole sense of identity is now thrown up in the air.

We all know that the older we get, the harder it is to learn new skills, to break old habits and to form new norms. It just takes longer and more discipline because over time we have become used to what works for us. That stands true for adjusting culture in an organization.

I am not prescribing that you simply leave everyone to carry on doing their own thing and allowing the current norms to linger; far from it.

But don't start out pointing the finger at people for being wrong, or for perpetuating a 'bad' culture. And do empathise that for some, it will take longer to shift than for others. Over time, as updated expectations are developed, communicated, repeated, reinforced, incentivised and so on, then if people still don't shift, that's when action can be taken. But never make culture personal. It's about behaviour, not about the human beings themselves. Always keep the two distinct.

Step away from the edge

There can be occasions when you are the one who should call for the work to stop, because it simply isn't the right context in which to carry it out. It takes courage and it can feel as if you have failed. But it is more of a success to prevent work being done that you know will fail; whether it is because the leadership just isn't willing to commit in the right way, or because the organization may be in a state of flux for some reason, or because the market has shifted totally and strategy needs to be the priority. There are any number of conditions under which this could be the case. You may well be quite deeply into the work. Don't pile on simply because you started. Since an organizational culture has no end date, there is no hard and fast deadline by which you have to tune in or to 'complete'. So, don't continue purely because you've been asked to. Remember, you are the one with the clearest picture of what is really going on and are therefore best placed to know when a break is required, or a slow-down. I missed this opportunity twice, and only when I led the work at a third attempt did I appreciate the moments when I should have called it.

Case Study – Back from the brink

I was working with an educational provider and services company that had hired external consultants to conduct a review of its culture. It was named as a 'culture audit' (note: what you call this work can have an impact on views of what should happen next). I was asked to take a look at the report, the proposed plan and to guide the top team through the next steps.

The work was great; thorough and insightful. But, in my view, there were two limitations to the assessment and proposed next steps:

- The gap the report outlined in the culture today was versus the expected culture, and did not include the strategy as well (which had altered since the culture was outlined). So there was a risk that the gap stated was versus something now outdated. Strengthening certain areas might not be necessary; conversely, given the revised strategy, certain strengths might need to be further honed.
- The proposed plan to close the gaps outlined workstreams, initiatives, a timeline, and every other piece of terminology that I have argued in this book creates a sense of shifting culture being a 'project' conducted by 'someone else' and 'done to' the organization.

Everyone was itching to assign people, to get moving and to drive the improvement. It was assumed that the report's proposed plan would be taken as the checklist of activity that would be followed. This showed me that the very first thing to do was indeed to slow everything down and to create a bit of a hiatus.

Management was passionate about focusing on the culture, and its criticality to the operating model and sustained performance, but their language was about 'them' not about 'us'.

It was clear they hadn't yet appreciated their impact on the culture as it was today, how to think about culture and strategy as symbiotic, and thereby whether the culture as they had stated it today was still appropriate or whether it needed clarifying or even adjusting.

So the guidance I provided back was to stop any and all further work immediately until:

- management had shared with employees (many of whom had been invited to share their views of the culture today) the report's findings on the current culture, that it would take time as management to really understand their impact and the impact the revising strategy would have on next steps.
- management could get a date in the diary to spend together and look in the mirror.

This met with resistance from some: wasn't this an audit, and therefore surely the recommended actions had to be closed out or else they would remain as open items? How could a culture audit be done and then no one put a plan in place? Don't we need to get on and fix it? Let's get some workstreams going and have someone in HR own it. We now have a report that says the culture has some weaknesses – we need to address them. The strategy is changing and the culture needs to line up to support it. Let's get on with it, otherwise we are wasting time.

Not only was the wave of enthusiasm to leap into action without pausing for breath the wrong thing to do, this also came at a time when there was significant turbulence in the external context around issues that the organization had no control over, that had not yet stabilised but would impact the way it needed to work. Finally, the company had also just taken the decision to diversify its business and grow in new areas, so the strategy was emerging and not yet finalised. This was just not the right moment to 'close the gap' on the culture when it wasn't clear yet what would be required.

However, faced with this wave of enthusiasm for getting into action on culture, meant that merely providing examples of where leaping into action to 'solve the problem' had been counter-productive was not going to convince them to slow up. Instead, I asked them to each send back to me the answer to the following questions:

- How do you define culture?
- How much of a shift in today's culture needs to happen to deliver the strategy into the future?
- What's your role in managing culture?

I collated their answers and presented them back to them as one picture; a very inconsistent picture around definition, ambition and their role. It helped. They recognised they weren't agreed on what problem they were trying to solve (yet they had assumed they were), they had differing ambitions based on how developed the strategy was in their own minds and they certainly hadn't yet really come to terms with how a culture is so impacted by their own tone.

We slowed up. We met once the key strategic focus areas were landed. We agreed the sorts of cultural traits that would then be essential, and went from there, following the overall process I outlined in Part Three, Chapter 11). Employees were enrolled in the process through culture 'jams', top leadership dedicated time to really listening and rolling up their sleeves in working sessions. Millions of dollars saved on external resources, diverted employee resource and activity that would have taken place in a maelstrom of unfolding context.

An amicable divorce

The most senior leader in the organization is not, by definition, the expected culture. Culture should endure from before their time and beyond their time. They are merely steering the ship for a while; but the ship sails on. However, they cast the longest shadow on it, and have the authority to review and redefine it; that cannot and should not be denied. This relationship can become a complicated one, and as the air-traffic controller, you have a birds-eye view of this. For some situations, it can indeed bring into sharp relief that this particular leader will struggle to lead the organization through to the next stage of its culture. Their intent around the culture required to deliver the strategy may be laudable and palpable, but it can run into trouble if they can't adjust their style towards it, and when it does, your role may be to call it out: not to the whole team, but quietly with that leader.

That may result in you having to stop the work. It may be that you can go no further. Be true to yourself and the work.

Finding a way to create an amicable divorce is more productive for the organization in the long run, than battling on trying to gain momentum, align the system and tap into people's energy around the culture if the leader simply cannot live out the culture that they know they need.

For example, a leader who has been exceptional in a crisis and powerfully embedded the culture required to engender a team effort to pull itself out of a particular hole, just may not be able to shape and lead a culture of consistent performance, or growth. They may have been able to take the impossible decisions, lead with grit under pressure, retain the best people, build energy around a focused goal and so on. But when the dust clears, and the organization returns to calmer waters and shifts towards growth, that same pugnacious, purposeful, singular focus that has been the leader's hallmark may be the very blocker to a culture of growth. That culture could require experimentation, challenge, adaptability, and employing some people who are deliberately disruptive to test the boundaries. Can that leader adjust to role-model what's now required? Maybe they can, but maybe they can't. But no one is likely to let them know that. And it can happen to the most influential of all – take Winston Churchill losing the UK General Election of 1945 right after the end of the Second World War. The public voted that their wartime leader wasn't the right one for peacetime. Organizations don't tend to have general elections. But in your role leading this work, you may have to find the right moment to be honest, and to exit stage left if they won't listen or try something different by admitting to the organization that they recognise their traits and struggle to adapt to what they know is needed and are asking others to exhibit.

I am not suggesting that you pile in and tell the most senior leader to resign – let's just get that clear! (that's for the board or whoever their bosses are to decide.) But, you are providing them with food for thought and an honesty that you can only take the work so far if their personal style cannot adjust towards the culture they are asking for.

Don't hide behind culture

Don't use culture as a substitute for setting clear purpose, direction, vision and strategy. I have said often in this book that culture and strategy should be treated as equals. But remember that culture is there to enable and underpin strategy, in support of purpose, direction and vision: not to provide a substitute for lack of clarity. You can't rely on creating growth purely because you've called for it and you focus on driving cultural traits that enable growth. There needs to be clear definition of what growth means, examples of what that looks like. Don't just hope that by having a culture that you need, it'll do the job for you of driving the performance delivery if it is not already defined. It has to be set in the context of what successful overall performance looks like: which means you have to have that clearly defined, and to keep sharing that context and the culture within it. I've been involved in this situation, and the push on a growth culture without a strategy created a situation of frustration and somewhat aimless activity. There was no clear funnel into which all this experimentation and new energy was channelled, as individuals and small teams created their own sense of what growth looked like and meant. In the end, morale slumped. Vision and strategy must be defined more than simply a direction, for the focus on culture to add value.

Look after yourself

This role is unbelievably fulfilling (well, I find it so). If your role is set up well, you have enormous influence, but you have very little decision-making authority. It can be frustrating, it can be exhausting and it can be an emotional rollercoaster. Yet you have to keep your passion and energy up for all those stakeholders who regard you as the lynchpin for the culture.

So who's looking after you? And how are you looking after yourself? Find some outlet valves in people you trust to offload around. If they are colleagues inside the organization, be sure they really are a confidante before you turn to them. Your public persona across the organization needs to be maintained. But be sure to find ways to step back occasionally and do something completely different. Take care of yourself, because quite often in this sort of role you find yourself 'taking care' of the organization, given the number of people who you may end up listening to.

My favourite boss from the US said that when it all got too much for him, he would take off and play a round of golf. When he returned, everything seemed a lot more straightforward. For me, it's a morning workout, retail therapy, chocolate, blueberries and red wine, a bath, and a period drama TV boxset. Not necessarily in that order. People often asked me how I kept my energy up and kept positive. I had my safety valves, as above. And, as a bottom line I was passionate about the work.

Whatever floats your boat. But find a boat to float.

You're never done

But remember you are never fully done. Even if it's not you who is working with the leaders anymore, 'stopping culture work' is folly, because the culture will simply develop in any case, just randomly. It'll be more of a lucky dip, and you'll get what you get.

I'll go right back to the beginning here. Culture should be considered with the same focus as strategy. You don't do it once and then forget about it. You don't call it an initiative or an intervention. You don't put it as AOB on the agenda. You don't make decisions and only then take a look to see if that fits with what you said was important. You don't treat it as an add-on to getting work done. As with strategy, it is the foundation of what's driving business decisions. It's the same with cars or house maintenance.

Case Study – A constant focus on culture to ensure continued alignment

---

An American technology services company noticed a slight dilution in their culture, through the consistent process by which they survey employees. Employee feedback was not as positive as it had been.

They responded fast, setting up workshops to talk about values and what they meant in action for employees. They wanted to hear how they experienced them and the way they were led.

Due to what they heard from the workshops, they created a summit, involving 1300 people, their entire population of people leaders, gathered in one place. The entire summit focused on culture, led by the executive team, and discussing why they work the way they do at the company and the business outcomes they expect to see as part of that. They invited comments on great and disappointing aspects of leadership in the company, honing in on issues via storytelling.

During the two days, the plenary sessions presented examples of real issues and asked the colleagues via an app, to select one of the options as to how they would deal with it. A member of the executive team then shared the results in the room and talked through how they would like to see the issue worked through when aligned with the values. The transparency the app results created in the room and the storytelling from the executive to share the expected approach, helped to re-set consistency across the people leadership of how the values should really come to life in that company.

What I have written in this book is a manual for getting started thinking about culture as a core part of your business performance, or when it needs an injection of focus beyond what is there today; when things are off track whether due to the expectations no longer lining up with strategy and context, or because they are not being followed – or both.

But just because you have got to grips with it now, don't be under any illusion that this will never be required again. It will; to some greater or lesser extent. Just like strategy.

Back to the four stages of competence, where it's all about learning skills and maintaining them. If the organization becomes too comfortable with its own culture and stops focusing on it overtly or reflecting on what it needs to adjust, it can become complacent, sloppy and slip into habits that mean it needs a stronger intervention down the line. It flips from Unconscious Competence (the Sunny Uplands where culture and strategy are aligned in theory and reality) to Unconscious Incompetence. Back to the analogy with driving. After a while, no matter how experienced you may be, we all slip slowly into a few bad habits of our own making.

You may not need a full-time air-traffic controller for culture, but I would propose that there is someone who has stewardship and responsibility for ensuring the focus and consistency remains. As I have said before in this book, most organizations have a lead Strategy role. That doesn't mean the strategy is always being redefined, but it does mean someone is constantly overseeing progress, providing regular updates and reviews and scanning the overall context to ensure it remains relevant. Why would you not bother for Culture?

So every year have a review of your culture's status and remind yourselves of what's vital.

Then every few years, take a deeper look to check whether:

1   It's what you thought it was.

2   It's what you need it to be.

Adjust accordingly, and repeat.

At a glance

A test of endurance

Culture within culture

Crisis drives candour

Choose alignment over satisfaction

Work with what you have to shift it

It's all a balancing act

Worse before better

No finger-pointing

Step away from the edge

An amicable divorce

Don't hide behind culture

Look after yourself

You're never done.

PART FIVE

BOOK ON A PAGE

If you read nothing else, this is what it all boils down to:

- **Culture and strategy are partners** not rivals: treat them as such, and focus on them equally.

- **Behavioural economics** is the core thinking here: faced with the same information, people won't always do what seems 'logical'. Accept baggage exists.

- **Alignment**, alignment, alignment: more important than content. If what's really going on doesn't match the expectations then it doesn't matter how funky the words are.

- **Fools rush in**: take time to be clear on the problem to solve. Is it changing today's culture, or changing the expectations, or both? Upfront navel-gazing is essential.

- **Asymptotic long-term maintenance**: you never get there and you're never done, because context always shifts and human beings are all different, not machines.

- **System shift and changing habits** not quick-fixes: a long term performance improvement comes from re-tuning the engine, optimising the fuel and ensuring they work well together, not slamming the foot on the accelerator.

- **Air-traffic control** not the pilot: the change lead orchestrates the organization to make the shift, rather than controlling and distributing activity. Your job is to set and operate the parameters for the skies to be safe, not to fly all the planes.

- **Red threads** have different thicknesses: the more common your operating model, the more consistent your culture should be.

PART SIX

EPILOGUE

Opportunity of a lifetime

Focusing on culture whether informally early in my career, formally in my later executive career or as a company director has proved to be the underpinning of what I have been able to achieve in business. And that is clearly aside from the advisory business I have created out of that very topic.

I am forever in debt to the people who believed in me to make career choices so I could focus further on culture as a core business driver. They are in the list of Acknowledgements, and they know exactly who they are.

People who thought I was sane making the choices I was, were few and far between in the early days, and to this day there are those who continue to tell me what's good for my career. Many managers, colleagues and mentors over the last couple of decades have expressed their concern and worries to me about my decision to focus here, citing that they feared I wouldn't be able to achieve my potential in business if I didn't dedicate more overt time to 'commercial leadership'.

What they really mean is, why didn't I just focus on the numbers? All well-meant, but dare I say, missing the point. That's exactly what I'm doing and have been doing all along – focusing on the numbers, but just looking further up the chain of root cause as to what's driving them to be weak or strong. It depends on how people behave, ultimately, as to whether there is success or failure. I don't do this work to make people happy or feel comfortable; I do this work to get to the root of better performance outcomes for the organization as a whole. It's untidy, it's messy, sometimes intangible or hidden beneath the surface: don't confuse that with commercial or wider performance irrelevance. Just because you can't quantify it, doesn't mean it isn't crucial.

For as long as there are people in the most senior positions who think culture work is stuff and nonsense, then that's a very reason why the sort of work I do is required. Once business schools put culture at the core of their teaching, once all CEOs put culture at the same level of focus as strategy, once investors truly use company culture as a measure in their analysis, then such guides as these won't be needed. It's not an overnight flick of a switch, but I see signs it's starting to happen and it's becoming more mainstream to ask the difficult questions on this topic.

Fact, fiction or hearsay

The examples I have provided in the book are a real mixture of observations of other organizations and my own experience where I have led or consulted on the work. They are naturally somewhat BP-heavy, with my twenty-four years there and the work I led post the Deepwater Horizon accident. But hopefully you can see sufficient examples from other organizations to give you assurance that this is not the story of one organization's culture shift, but a more generic overview of what it takes.

In some cases I have named the organization where I think it is appropriate. In others, I have left it more generic, for good reasons, as this is not a book critiquing the efforts of particular companies to manage or shift their culture but an illustration of the processes it takes to do just that. It is a handbook for anyone who is leading this sort of work. As such, there are instances where I did not deem it appropriate to share the organization's name. If any of those involved is reading this, you know who you are and what organization you are part of, but it's not for me to share that. However, every single one of these instances has happened, and it is the way I, or someone I interviewed dealt with it. Nothing is made up, nothing is theoretical.

PART SEVEN

ACKNOWLEDGEMENTS

My own stakeholders – for the book, for this work

Norma – for teaching me how to think and do things differently. I learnt so much from you and am eternally in your debt for your partnership.

Becky – for that meeting in 2007 that started this whole thing off. Sixth floor, floral shift dress, big belt.

Margaret – for drip-feeding me the sense of confidence and need to write this book. The Chiltern Firehouse will forever be our place.

Iain – for believing in me, shoving me forward as a leader and respecting (if not always agreeing with) my instincts – always. And for the best chats over red wine.

Steve – for not letting me resign, when I didn't really want to anyway. I just needed you to listen and respect my choices; and you did. So, I was able to do this work.

Ross – for providing me with the best 'look in the mirror' moment at work in 2002. The best honest feedback ever given to me. It was a joy to work with you every day. Forever a top boss.

Karen – Winter Palace, St Petersburg 2007: need I say more. It opened my mind to what I could really do.

Cliff – skull t-shirt, 'suits from Head Office' – bring it on. Yet, she persisted. Our partnership helped change the game with the front line and I will value it forever. Never stop speaking at that speed.

Bev – a team for 8 years. We got a lot done.

Hayden – Missy always did listen to your wise Aussie counsel.

Ed – a wee bit of a partner in crime.

St Catharine's College, Cambridge – for not having a resident tutor in Anglo-Saxon, Norse and Celtic in 1987 when I applied. If you had, I would never have picked Economics as my degree and this book might well have been a dissertation on Icelandic sagas (interesting in itself but perhaps with a different readership).

Colleagues across BP – so many of the examples I use in this book are from my experience of leading this work at BP. I worked there for twenty-four years; it was everything I knew in terms of corporate experience for the first half of my career and it's where I learned how to conduct this sort of work. But more than that, the individuals who were change agents, wise heads when I sought advice, simply an ear when I needed someone to talk to when I was feeling exhausted by this work, sponsors and mentors across the full twenty-four years, ensured it was such a rich experience and place to learn all I know today. As I write this book at forty-eight, it lasted half of my entire life to date. I'll always, always treasure my time there and my chance to work around the world in such a vital industry.

… and Hattie – one coffee, 4 ideas and here we are. Not possible without you. Thank you.

INDEX